This book is published strictly for historical purposes.
The Naval and Military Press Ltd
expressly bears no responsibility or liability of any type,
to any first, second or third party, for any harm,
injury or loss whatsoever.

Elliott & Fry] [*Photo.*
CAPT. W. EDGEWORTH-JOHNSTONE.

CHAMPIONSHIP SERIES.

BOXING

THE

MODERN SYSTEM OF GLOVE FIGHTING

BY

CAPT. W. EDGEWORTH-JOHNSTONE,
Royal Irish Regiment,
ASSISTANT INSPECTOR OF GYMNASIA.
HEAVY-WEIGHT AMATEUR CHAMPION OF ENGLAND,
1895 AND 1896.

The Naval & Military Press Ltd

Published by

The Naval & Military Press Ltd
Unit 5 Riverside, Brambleside
Bellbrook Industrial Estate
Uckfield, East Sussex
TN22 1QQ England

Tel: +44 (0)1825 749494

www.naval-military-press.com
www.nmarchive.com

*In reprinting in facsimile from the original, any imperfections are inevitably reproduced
and the quality may fall short of modern type and cartographic standards.*

INTRODUCTION.

I have been induced to bring this book before the public in the hope that it may lead to our amateurs adopting a more practical form of Boxing, and also that some of our professionals may think it worth their while to study more closely American methods of training and fighting.

I may add that my own knowledge of Boxing, and any successes I may have had, are entirely due to the careful instruction of Professor T. Burrows.

I have to acknowledge the courtesy of the Editor of *Sandow's Magazine* for permitting me to re-publish the special articles at the end of the book, viz.: those on "Boxing in the Army," "American *versus* English Boxers," "The Knock-out Blow," and "Physical Culture at Public Schools," together with illustrations.

The photographs of professionals are published by kind permission of the Editor of *The Mirror of Life*, and four of the boxing pictures by that of the Editor of *The Navy and Army Illustrated.*

I have to thank Mr. Bettinson and Mr. Dunning for many useful hints, photographs, and records of professionals.

W. EDGEWORTH-JOHNSTONE.

Dedicated

TO

COLONEL G. M. FOX,

INSPECTOR OF GYMNASIA.

CONTENTS.

	PAGE
POSITION "ON GUARD"	8
,, OF HANDS	10
"LEADING"	17
LEFT HAND "LEAD" AT HEAD	18
RIGHT ,, ,, ,, ,,	22
LEFT ,, ,, ,, BODY	26
RIGHT ,, ,, ,, ,,	26
DOUBLE "LEADS"	29
"COUNTERING"	30
LEFT HAND "COUNTER" AT HEAD	34
,, ,, ,, ,, BODY	37
RIGHT ,, ,, ,, HEAD	37
,, ,, ,, ,, BODY	38
,, ,, "CROSS COUNTER" ("KNOCK-OUT BLOW")	38
LEFT HAND "CROSS COUNTER"	42
"IN FIGHTING"	45
"CLINCHING"	49
"GUARDING"	50
"RING" TACTICS	53
TRAINING FOR BOXING	70
THE PUNCHING BALL	81
THE MEDICINE BAG	83
JUDGING	84
THE NATIONAL SPORTING CLUB	90
BOXING IN THE ARMY	105
AMERICAN BOXERS v. ENGLISH	131

	PAGE
THE "KNOCK-OUT BLOW"	139
PHYSICAL CULTURE AT PUBLIC SCHOOLS	146
GEORGE (KID) LAVIGNE	152
PEDLAR PALMER	154
FRANK CRAIG (THE COFFEE COOLER)	156
BOB FITZSIMMONS	158
AMES J. JEFFRIES	160
TOM SHARKEY	162
BOXING RULES OF THE NATIONAL SPORTING CLUB	165

LIST OF ILLUSTRATIONS.

	PAGE
CAPTAIN W. EDGEWORTH-JOHNSTONE	*Frontispiece*
LEFT "LEAD"	5
LEFT "STOP"	11
,, "COUNTER"	15
,, "HOOK"	19
,, "STOP"	23
,, "BODY COUNTER"	27
RIGHT "COUNTER" OR "STOP"	31
,, "BODY COUNTER"	35
,, HAND "CROSS COUNTER"	39
,, ,, ,, ,, (BLOW COMPLETED)	43
,, ,, ,, ,, ("KNOCKED OUT")	47
LEFT HAND "CROSS COUNTER"	51
"HAMMER BLOW"	55
"SLING CHANGE"	59
A "CLINCH"	63
LEFT ARM "GUARD"	67
DOUBLE "GUARD"	71
RIGHT HAND "UPPER CUT"	75
PUNCHING BALL IN POSITION	79
TOM SAYERS	85
MR. J. FLEMING	91
MR. A. F. BETTINSON	95
MR. J. B. ANGLE	99
MR. G. DUNNING	103
BOXING FOR THE ARMY CHAMPIONSHIP	107

LIST OF ILLUSTRATIONS

	PAGE
COLONEL G. M. FOX	111
CORPORAL SMITH	119
STAFF-SERGEANT SINGLETON	123
MR. TOM BURROWS	127
CROCKET	137
GEORGE (KID) LAVIGNE	153
PEDLAR PALMER	155
FRANK CRAIG	157
BOB FITZSIMMONS	159
JAMES J. JEFFRIES	161
TOM SHARKEY	163

BOXING.

———>•<———

There are two points of view from which Boxing may be considered, one as an interesting and effective form of healthy exercise, the other as a practical means of self-defence. It is the latter, and more serious, aspect that I intend to deal with.

The majority of amateur boxers are "sparrers" pure and simple; the majority of boxing professors teach nothing but sparring. This is partly the fault of the amateur, and partly that of the professor. There can be no doubt that most amateurs devote their leisure time to learning the art with a view to self-defence, yet they rarely acquire much knowledge likely to be of practical value to them in an emergency.

The reasons for this state of things are, I think, simple enough.

The beginner, disliking drudgery, wants to get on to loose play at once, and, as the fees of the professor depend upon pleasing the pupil, he usually succeeds. Consequently, he misses the whole ground-work of the art, which is hitting—hitting quickly, heavily and accurately. If an apt pupil, he becomes proficient in ducking, dodging, and light flippy hitting, and may eventually out-point his professor at this game. He has become, in fact, an elegant "sparrer," but has not, as the pros. say, "a decent punch in him." He is, however, quite satisfied that he is pretty useful, goes into training, enters for a competition, and, if he runs up against a hitter, gets knocked out in the first round. This will, indeed, be a blessing in disguise, if it induces him to study the practical side of the art. But only a small proportion of amateurs enter for competitions, and, failing to find their level, many go through life under the comfortable delusion that they are dangerous fellows to meddle with. Many, unhappily, experience a rude awakening at the hands of some unskilled brawny ruffian. The boxing professor, who is frequently a respectable elderly gentleman, cannot, I suppose, be held responsible; business is business; he must please his pupils, and the labour of teaching hearty young novices to hit, is far greater, and far less pleasant, than teaching them to spar.

It is important to recognise that no amount of science can compensate for the lack of hitting power, and powerful hitting is terribly discounted, unless it is well timed, accurate, and rapid.

I am firmly convinced that the first step for a beginner is learning to hit properly with either hand. If he once masters this difficult accomplishment, he can, without any further instruction what-

PRELIMINARY

ever, dispose of any " sparring " gentleman or unskilled opponent with the utmost ease.

To make anything like rapid progress, the pupil must have constant practice at the swinging punching ball and the medicine bag (see pages 81 and 83), under the supervision of an expert; simple foot work, such as advancing and retiring, being taught in conjunction with hitting.

It is important to note that the effectiveness of a severe punch is derived from the sudden bracing of the leg extensor muscles, which push the weight forward; the swing of the body from the hips, and the extension of the shoulders, which carry it on, adding intensity, and, finally, the rapid extension of the arm, which conducts it "home."

These movements are successive, and may be compared to the tributaries of a river. An arm blow has, in itself, little force, the only muscle brought into serious play being the triceps.

The instructor should commence by teaching his pupil simple "leads." He should never parry them in the ordinary manner, or avoid them by ducking. The pupil must be taught to lunge well out, and allow his blows to get well home before recovering. When "leading" at the face, the instructor should turn his head to the right, receiving the blow on the open palm, turning the padded back towards his own face for protection. When at the body, the pupil should be directed to "lead" at the instructor's glove, placed over the required spot, palm next the body. Flipping, snatchiness, and "leading" short, are bad habits, only too readily acquired, and are, as a rule, the result of an injudicious display of cleverness on the part of the professor.

When teaching "countering," the instructor's "leads" should be slow at first, and the pupil's "counters" should be allowed to land on the glove ; by this means an instructor can always gauge the accuracy and sting of the hits.

Having been taught to "lead and counter" effectively, the next step is "feinting." This is a most important branch of pugilistic education, and much time and trouble must be devoted to it. It is, unfortunately, too much neglected, not only by amateurs, but by some of our best professionals, who have had many severe lessons from our Yankee cousins in the art of " creating an impression."

"Guarding," "ducking," "side slipping," and "advanced footwork," come last. When these are thoroughly mastered, little remains, as far as the instructor is concerned, beyond some hints on "Ring" tactics and training. Further progress will depend upon natural ability and experience. Loose play should never be indulged in until the pupil has been thoroughly grounded in the above. Very little loose play is advisable when training for a competition. Besides the risks of a swollen nose, a black eye, or a sprained wrist, it leads to bad habits, as, if it

"LEFT LEAD."

(Instructor's Guard.)

[*See page 4.*

takes the form of sparring, a complete alteration of style is necessary, unless some kind friend is willing to lend his vile body for knocking-out practice.

It is well to remember that a hitter can always descend to sparring for amusement and exercise, but a sparrer cannot turn on a punching tap if suddenly let in for real business.

Most professors waste too much time in teaching what they call "style." As a pupil passes from the rudimentary stage, he will naturally acquire a style of his own, and this, if not absolutely vicious, should not be corrected. His strong points should be carefully noted and developed for all they are worth, and his weak points discounted by adopting the mode of fighting best calculated to cover them.

Boxing instructors should bear in mind the fact that most men possess two hands, and that of these two the right is the stronger and the more accurate. This advice may appear superfluous, but I still hear the old moth-eaten dogma impressed on the beginner—"Hit with the left and guard with the right." No advice could possibly be more misleading, or more opposed to common sense. A restricted use of the right hand is, to my mind, the principal fault of English boxers, both amateur and professional. Of course, a good deal of parrying must be done with the right hand, but, in dealing with beginners, it is far preferable to impress on them the superiority of the "duck and counter" over the "guard and return."

POSITION "ON GUARD."

I AM not a believer in laying down any hard and fast rule as to the man's position when "on guard."

Amongst first class professionals, there are hardly two who stand alike.

Each individual gradually adopts the pose which he finds by experience is best suited to his own style of fighting.

Still, there are certain principles which should be observed, and these, in a general way, must be laid down for beginners to work upon.

The weight of the body should be fairly evenly balanced on the legs, with, perhaps, a shade more weight thrown on the rear leg.

The width of the stride will depend on the individual's length of limb : if it is too short, there is a loss of stability ; if too wide, a loss of mobility.

The happy medium can only be found by constant practice and experience ; roughly, this would be about two-and-a-quarter times the length of the foot.

The legs should be sufficiently bent, *i.e.*, their muscles sufficiently contracted to permit of a sudden spring in any direction, the weight of the body being carried chiefly on the fore part of the feet; the trunk should be turned partly sideways. This position has the advantage of—

(1) Presenting a small target.
(2) Withdrawing the " mark."

POSITION "ON GUARD"

(3) Leaving the right hand in the most favourable position for delivering a blow.

The left shoulder should be held higher than the right, to protect the jaw, and the chin slightly drawn in, for the same purpose.

The hands should move with a quiet backward and forward swing, elbows close to the body. They should be loosely closed, backs uppermost. The left hand forearm and elbow horizontal, the right hand protecting the "mark," the eyes fixed on the adversary's.

How often one sees in England amateurs and professionals adopting a stiff ungainly pose. This usually takes the form of keeping the left hand very far advanced, both hands tightly clenched, the feet very wide apart, the rear leg very much bent, and almost all the weight of the body thrown on it; this position is frequently supplemented by wild extravagant motions of the arms. What is worse still, the same pose exactly is maintained throughout a competition or contest, except when actually avoiding an attack or delivering one. The maintenance of an unvarying pose is extremely tiring (as are superfluous movements of the arms). It allows no latitude for a surprise hit, and permits the process of "sizing up" to be completed very rapidly by a cute opponent. Nothing bothers an adversary more than variety, both in attack and defence, and it eases the physical strain by constantly shifting the onus of exertion from one group of muscles to another. Frequent opportunities should be taken of dropping the hands, and relaxing everything when out of distance.

POSITION OF HANDS.

THE exact position of the hands when hitting may seem a small matter so long as the blows " arrive " all right. But, in reality, it is a very important consideration.

In the days of the prize ring, when fights lasted for hours, and the " knock-out " blow was unknown, the condition of a man's hands was all-important. Heenan would, in all probability, have defeated Sayers, but for the swollen condition of his hands.

The prize fighter's hands were his special care; they were pickled in brine to make them tough, and specially manipulated to make them strong; further than this, the men were trained to hit with the hands in a disadvantageous and tiring position, in order that the large knuckles should always take the shock. There was probably another reason. Where " knock-outs " were not thought of, it was good policy to cut the opponent's face and body as much as possible, and for this purpose the bony projections of the large knuckles are eminently adapted. But now, when the protecting

"LEFT STOP."
(For "Right Hand Lead.")

[See page 34.

glove is worn, such considerations fall to the ground.

At the present day, the majority of our boxing professors instruct their pupils to hit with their hands held in the old-fashioned manner, because, as I mentioned before, they teach "sparring" and not real business, and it is next door to impossible to deliver a light blow with the back of the hand turned up. Any man who learns to hit with the back of the hand turned down, places a serious check upon the vigour of his blows.

If you stand erect and allow the arms to hang down loosely by the sides, you will find that the backs of the hands naturally turn to the front, although not exactly parallel to it. Now bend the arms at the elbows until the forearms are at right angles to the upper arms, the back of the hands remain turned up, the large knuckle of the forefinger being the highest point, the forearms and hands are now in "pronation."

In order to turn the large knuckles down, a strong effort of the rotatory muscles of the forearms is necessary, and this effort must be maintained to keep the hands in this position, viz., that of "supination." This, in a competition, must be tiring. Again, it is well-known the accuracy with which a child even will point at an object. How does it hold the hand? With the forefinger extended, and the hand and forearm in "pronation." The same position is adopted when writing and painting, and, in fact, whenever the hand is used for accurate work.

Therefore, it is less tiring and more accurate to hit with the back of the hand turned up.

This is more or less theory, but it is confirmed in practice by the fact that all the Yankee boxers of note adopt this position of the hands when hitting at the head.

When hitting at the body, however, this position of the hands should not be adopted, because it has been found that the yielding nature of the target is liable to cause a sprained wrist; moreover, the target is large, and, therefore, there is not the same pressing need for accuracy.

When hitting at the body, the backs of the hands should be turned outwards, inner side of wrists towards the body.

It is highly important that the hands and forearms should be well developed, as they are subjected to a severe strain, and a dislocated finger, or a sprained wrist, is likely to prove fatal to success. A simple and convenient exercise for effecting this is by opening and closing the fists rapidly with all the force possible. These movements should be continued until the hands and forearms are quite tired. An equally good method is to knead a small india-rubber ball, or a piece of paper, with the fingers and thumbs, in the palms of the hands. These exercises may be carried out at all kinds of odd moments—when out walking, for

"LEFT COUNTER."
(For "Left Lead at Head.")

[See page 34.

example, or during a railway journey. I remember once frightening an old lady when travelling up to London. I was holding a newspaper up with one hand, reading, and opening and shutting the other as hard as I could go ; happening to look up, I saw her eyes nervously fixed on the performing hand ; I think, however, the old lady scored most, because I confess I felt as foolish as a man caught talking to himself in a looking glass.

"LEADING."

THE majority of amateur competitions are won by quick left hand "leads"; the majority of professional contests by successful manœuvring for a "knock-out."

Most amateurs, being ignorant of the real art of hitting, devote all their energies to the development of light rapid "sparring." The bouts in a competition consist of three rounds only, so that it is necessary to bustle, many a competition being lost by waiting for an opportunity which never presents itself. Most important professional contests run to twenty rounds, which allow a man more margin for biding his time.

The man who stands on the defensive is deemed to hold an advantage. If both men try to adopt defensive or "countering" tactics, a poor contest is the result. To prevent this, and to discount the waiting game, in all contests or competitions where the points are about equal, the decision goes to the man who has done the most "leading." It therefore pays better, as a general rule, especially in amateur competitions, to be aggressive.

To minimise the danger of being heavily "countered," "leads" with either hand should almost always be preceded by a "feint" of some sort, that is, by a movement which deceives the opponent as to the real point of attack, and induces him to uncover that portion of his anatomy which it is intended to visit.

A "feint," to be of any use, must be full of "expression," so as to create the impression that it is a real attack. It may be described as a real attack minus the final movement. A mere motion of the arm alone will have little or no effect; it is the sudden and combined motions of the whole body, together with the expression of the face, that deceives an adversary.

LEFT HAND "LEAD" AT HEAD.

THIS is the quickest offensive movement in Boxing, because the left hand is nearest the opponent's face, and has, consequently, the shortest road to travel. It can be effected without any preliminary or warning movement of the arm, and

"LEFT HOOK."
(For "Left Lead at Head.")

[*See page 34.*

entails little exertion; it is, therefore, justly popular, and a sure scorer of points.

It consists of a sharp forward lunge with the left leg, accompanied by a rapid extension of the left arm. It is rarely a severe blow, but, in addition to its "run-getting" qualities, it is a useful preliminary to a right hand swing, and should be delivered with the back of the hand up.

In delivering this "lead," the position of the head should be constantly varied, sometimes up, sometimes down, and sometimes "neither up nor down." Security against a "head counter" may be attained by leading with the right hand in front of the face. This will, however, entail a loss of reach and rapidity.

I can illustrate the danger of not varying the position of the head when "leading," by an experience of my own.

In the Amateur Championships, 1895, in the first bout of the heavy-weight, I was opposed by a tall Birmingham man, who commenced hostilities by "leading" at my head with his left four times in rapid succession. Each "lead" was delivered in exactly the same way, with the head well up. He landed the first, but I "cross-countered" him heavily with my right on each of the last three. This practically finished the bout. The rapidity of the result was entirely due to a want of simple common sense on his part.

The left "lead" at head may be preceded by a

left "feint" at body, a right "feint" at head or body, or by a left "feint" at head, followed rapidly by a left "lead" at head.

There is another form of left "lead" at head, which, if more difficult to bring off, is infinitely more effective. This is a hook blow directed at the chin. It is, however, easier to accomplish as a "counter" than as a "lead." As it can only be brought off at fairly close range, it is necessary to step in before delivering it. The left arm must be kept well bent at the elbow, back of the hand up. The blow is delivered in an upward direction, and its chief force is derived from a body swing from left to right, assisted by a sudden bracing up of the legs. It is most likely to be successful with an opponent who persists in raising his right elbow when guarding his face. In this case, the left hand, passing between his right arm and body, lands beneath the chin. It should be followed instantly by a right hand punch at the jaw.

Tom Tracy knocked out Tom Williams at the National Sporting Club in the first round with these two hits; they were the only blows struck.

RIGHT HAND "LEAD" AT HEAD.

THIS is the most dangerous "lead" of all, and, if attempted at all carelessly, merely courts disaster; it exposes everything. The right hand has such a

"LEFT STOP."
(For "Left Lead at Body.")

[*See page* 37.

RIGHT HAND "LEAD" AT HEAD

long distance to travel, that the opponent gets an easy chance of "countering" straight with the left, and, if he can anticipate the movement by the fraction of a second, of bringing off a "knock-out" on the left side of the chin with his right.

It can, however, be often successfully accomplished if preceded by a really good "feint" at the body with the left, especially if the opponent has recently received a left-hander on the body. The "feint," if properly executed, will bring his hands down and expose the head. It must be carried out very rapidly, and without any hesitation.

It is not, however, to be recommended to a beginner, except when confronted with an exhausted or indifferent boxer.

It is more likely to be successful at close quarters, and, if it is attempted without a "feint," the left hand should be thrown across lower portion of face, hand open, palm downwards; in delivering it, the back of the right hand should be uppermost; the danger in bringing it off is somewhat compensated for by its effectiveness, if successful.

In the memorable fight between Kid Lavigne and Dick Burge, at the National Sporting Club, Lavigne constantly led with the right. Burge stands with his left hand very much to the front, and each time Lavigne led he placed his left on top of Burge's left. He got home safely every time, Burge never seeming to tumble to the dodge.

LEFT HAND "LEAD" AT BODY.

THIS is a form of attack which one sees constantly attempted by amateurs in a similar manner to that adopted in a left "lead" at the head, viz., merely a direct lunge without any swing. Of course, if this blow reaches, it scores a point, and it might possibly be used with advantage against an opponent who stands "square on" and very straight, but there is hardly any force in it. It exposes the attacker to the gravest danger, and is very liable to end in a sprained thumb or wrist. To be effective, it must be a short arm punch at fairly close quarters, in fact, almost a hook blow. It should be slightly round, so as to meet the opponent's body somewhere about the "mark." In carrying it out, it is necessary to step in, danger from a left hand upper-cut being avoided by throwing the right hand across the face, hand open and palm downwards. It is one of the most effective blows in boxing, and frequently results in a " knock out." It should be delivered with the back of the hand to the left, thumb uppermost, and may be preceded by a left or right " feint " at head.

RIGHT HAND "LEAD" AT BODY.

THIS blow is not so dangerous as the right hand "lead" at head. It consists of a short arm punch directed at the opponent's left side, just above

"LEFT BODY COUNTER."
(For "Left Lead at Head.")

[See page 37.

the hip bone. In delivering it, the arm should move close to the side, and to give it the maximum force, the body must be swung sharply from right to left. It may be preceded by a "feint" with the left at the face, if not, the left hand should be thrown across the lower part of face to guard against a right hand "upper-cut." It is necessary to step well in to deliver it, keeping the back of the hand to the right, thumb uppermost.

Mr. Joe Steers, of Amateur Championship fame, is an adept at this particular punch.

With an opponent who keeps his left hand very much to the front, this blow can often be successfully accomplished. The "dodge" is to knock his arm outwards with a sharp blow on his glove with the left hand; this exposes his left side; the punch must follow with lightning-like rapidity.

"DOUBLE LEADS.

"DOUBLE LEADS" are very effective, especially against a man who is slow on his feet, or who is exhausted. The best are—

(1) Left and right at head.
(2) Left and right at body.
(3) Left at head, and right at body.
(4) Left at body, and right at head.

The hits must follow in rapid succession, and should be carried out with a short rush.

One of the most favourable opportunities for a "double lead" is when the opponent is close to the ropes; the first hit is likely to drive him against them, and the second hit to catch him on the rebound. It is always safer to commence a "double lead" with the left hand.

"COUNTERING."

WELL-TIMED "counters" are the cause of nine-tenths of the "knock outs" in boxing, the right hand "cross-counter" being responsible for the lion's share.

The extra force of a "counter," compared with a "lead," is, of course, accounted for by the fact that the "counter" is delivered during the forward movement of an opponent when "leading."

A successful "lead" has only the attacker's weight behind it, but in a "counter," the weight of both men is concentrated in the fist of him who "counters."

It is much easier to teach the pupil to "lead" well, than to "counter" effectively, and most amateurs, and many professionals, are lamentably backward in this all-important branch of the "Noble Art."

A man, to "counter" well, must have a good eye, and be a nice judge of distance; he must, in addition be cool, quick, and accurate.

"RIGHT COUNTER OR STOP."
(For "Left Swing at Body.")

[*See page* 37.

Any active man can be taught to "lead" and "recover" with power and rapidity, because the motions are more or less mechanical, and he can choose his own time for starting the "machinery."

It is far different with "countering"; the "leader" chooses the time, and also that portion of his target about to be exposed. The man who "counters" is in a somewhat similar position to a boy who starts in a race at his opponent's word "go."

The attacker can make up his mind at leisure compared to the fraction of a second afforded to his opponent.

The "lead," a rapid movement, starts first, and after it has started, the poor chap waiting for his "counter" has to decide which side he is going to "duck," which hand he is going to use, and what he is going to aim for.

As a matter of fact, with a quick opponent who varies his attacks, all this cannot be done, and the man on the defensive must make up his mind beforehand what he is going to try for, and leave the result to chance.

With an opponent who is slow with his "leads," or who indulges in preliminary warning movements, or who lacks variety, a man who "counters" well can get home almost every time.

With two evenly-matched competitors, the advantage lies with the man who "counters," owing to the enormously increased severity of his blows. The process of drawing a man for a particular "lead," described under "Ring Tactics," does away with many of the difficulties of "countering," besides giving its exponent in the eyes of the judges the appearance of being the aggressor.

LEFT "COUNTER AT HEAD.

THIS "counter," if the least severe, is the safest and easiest to accomplish.

It is used on the opponent's right or left "lead" at head or body.

ON RIGHT "LEAD" AT HEAD.

Keeping the left shoulder well up, lower the head sideways to the right, so as to avoid any chance of the right landing, and hit straight at the chin; the body must come forward to put weight into the blow.

ON LEFT "LEAD" AT HEAD.

(*a*) Raising the right hand to parry the "lead," hit straight for the nose and mouth with the left.

(*b*) Ducking forward, and to the right, allow the opponent's "lead" to pass over the left shoulder, at the same time hitting straight for the face with the left. The "duck" must not be exaggerated, or the weight of the body will not be behind the arm.

(*c*) Ducking, as in (*b*), deliver left hand "hook" hit described under left hand "leads." This is

"Right Body Counter."
(For "Left Lead at Head.")

[See page 38.

especially effective against a man who "leads" with his head down, or who, when "leading," holds his right in front of his face.

On Left Hand "Lead" at Body.

Drawing in lower part of the trunk and hips, hit for the head with the left. This is a complete "stop" or time hit, as it will reach home long before the "lead," having a shorter distance to travel.

LEFT "COUNTER" AT BODY.

This is a desperately severe hit, if properly timed and accurately directed.

It is delivered on the opponent's left "lead" at head. It consists of the short arm punch before described under "Left 'Lead' at Body," and is accomplished by a rather low "duck" to the right to avoid the opponent's "lead," and to allow of a good swing from left to right on the hips. It should be frequently employed against an adversary who protects his face with the right hand when "leading" at the head with the left.

RIGHT "COUNTER" AT HEAD.

This is a very difficult "counter" to bring off, and one rarely sees it used.

But some men nowadays, especially second-rate professionals, adopt a faulty and unscientific method of "leading" with the left. This consists of round arm swings at the jaw, and upward swings at the body, the arm being held quite straight. To obtain the necessary momentum, they are obliged to start the swing by drawing the left shoulder very far back. This is the opportunity for the right hand "counter" or "stop," as the left side of the chin is fully exposed. The blow is a perfectly straight "jab" with the right.

RIGHT HAND "COUNTER AT BODY.

THIS is a most telling blow, and, curiously enough, seems to affect some men much more than others. It is delivered on the opponent's left " lead " at head, and consists of the short arm punch, described under "Right Hand 'Lead' at Body," the head being ducked low to the left.

RIGHT HAND "CROSS COUNTER
(KNOCK OUT BLOW).

THIS is, without exception, the most important blow in Boxing. In professional contests, the minds and energies of the combatants are per-

(1) RIGHT HAND "CROSS COUNTER."
("Knock-out" Blow, for "Left Lead at Head.")

[See page 38.

sistently devoted to its successful accomplishment. It is a most difficult blow to teach a beginner, and a very few Englishmen, amateur or professional, are good at it. The Americans have reduced it to a fine art, and it is most instructive to watch all the different ruses and devices they make use of to procure an opening for it.

The principal fault to guard against is making it a round blow. This fault is almost universal, and the reasons against it are, I think, conclusive.

In the first place, if it is made a round arm swing, the target (the opponent's head) becomes a moving target, and the blow may finish in front of or behind it, or it may meet the opponent's ear, *i.e.*, the centre of the target, approached from the side, as it would in a round arm swing. At any rate, the odds are against its finding the corner of the chin.

Again, directly the right elbow is raised outwards from the side, the hand moves in a half circle towards the object, while the weight of the body is going straight forward ; consequently, there is a break in the strong line of resistance which ought to exist between the rear foot and the right hand.

Again, the right hand is moving round the circumference of a circle, instead of across the diameter.

The blow should be delivered perfectly straight on the opponent's left "lead" at the face. The head must be ducked forward and to the left, to avoid the opponent's "lead," but the "duck" must be very slight, only just sufficient to avoid being hit. The right hand, back uppermost, should just skim the opponent's left elbow before his left arm is straightened, and the swing of the body on the hips from right to left should be assisted by jerking back the left elbow and shoulder. Thus we secure the three main factors in an effective punch :—

(*a*) Severity—because the weight of the body is directly behind the blow, and the opponent's head is coming forward to meet it.

(*b*) Rapidity—because the shortest road to the opponent's jaw is followed.

(*c*) Accuracy—because the target never deviates from the " line of fire," and must, if uncovered, be found at some range or other during its forward movement.

A special article upon this particular hit will be found further on, republished by kind permission of the Editor of " Sandow's Magazine."

LEFT HAND " CROSS COUNTER.

THIS is a bent arm swing with the left hand, delivered on the opponent's left " lead " at head. The left elbow must be raised outwards until in a line with the shoulder, and the head ducked forward and to the right. The blow is a round one, and is a useful variety ; it is very likely to get home outside the guard of a man, who, when " leading "

(2) RIGHT HAND "CROSS COUNTER."
(Blow completed)

[*See page 38.*

with the left, protects his face with the right hand. If it happens to catch the angle of the jaw, a "knock out" is not unlikely to be the result.

"IN-FIGHTING."

This is a branch of Boxing sadly neglected by the majority of bruisers.

One rarely sees a bout without a certain amount of "in-fighting" takes place, yet how few men ever dream of practising it ! The consequence is, one seldom comes across a clever "in-fighter." Directly men get close, a series of wild, inaccurate blows are sure to follow. A short, slow man, by persisting with this form of fighting, can discount enormously the extra reach and cleverness of a lengthy opponent. If ever one is called upon to fight in earnest, the struggle is almost certain to consist of "in-fighting." Few street rowdies will stand out and box in the ordinary manner. The blows in this form of Boxing consist of half-arm hits. The great object is to "hook" the opponent under the chin; with this end in view, the shoulders should be shrugged up and the chin sunk on the chest, and the arms, if possible, kept inside those of the opponent.

Hall, the Australian, was a wonderful "in-fighter," and practised assiduously the short-arm "hammer blow," with which he "knocked out" Slavin. (See illustration.)

To effect the "hammer blow" when "in-fighting," the right upper arm and elbow must be squeezed tight against the right side, and the blow delivered with the heel of the hand across the angle of the opponent's chin, the right elbow being used as a fulcrum.

There is a movement called in America a "sling change," which, perhaps, ought to be described under the head of "in-fighting."

When the opponent "leads" at the head with his left, duck well forward and to the right, and, as he recovers from the lunge, change feet by taking a long, rapid pace to the front with the right foot, driving the left at the mark or chin. This is a desperately severe punch, because the right foot is in front and the left hand drawn back, and, consequently, the blow is identical with the right hand punch, left foot in front.

It is most easily carried out by a short man when opposed to a big adversary. Mr. Alfred Bettinson, now manager of the National Sporting Club, reduced this hit to a fine art. It needs constant practice in hitting with the left hand, right foot in front.

(3) "KNOCKED-OUT."

[See page 38.

"CLINCHING."

It is not my intention to give any *hints* on this particular "art," because I am of opinion that "clinching" ought not to be allowed in Boxing at all, although, at the same time, I am quite aware of its advantages, as well as those of wrestling and even of kicking.

It is, perhaps, best described, by a seeming "bull," as "the art of holding without holding."

The principle of "clinching" is, that, having failed to stagger or drive back an opponent in the attack, and whilst "corps a corps" on the lunge, it is safer to remain close to him than to recover in the ordinary manner.

Men in a "clinch" do not actually hold one another in the ordinary sense with their hands, but they lie up against one another, and, to all intents and purposes, indulge in hugging, each one striving to give the other the exertion of pushing him away.

The American "cracks" are the worst sinners; so much so, that in America the referee is obliged to walk about inside the ropes for the purpose of forcing the men apart.

Most of the big fights consist from start to finish of a series of short rushes, followed by a "clinch." This may be clever and practical, as long as it does not entail disqualification, but it is not Boxing, and is very wearisome to the spectators.

"GUARDING."

"GUARDING" with the hands or arms should be indulged in as little as possible, every opportunity being taken to "duck" and "counter."

When a man is pressed, however, it becomes absolutely necessary to protect the face and body with the hands. The head is protected from a left "lead" by the right hand raised in front of the face, glove open, palm towards the opponent, and elbow kept down. A right hand "lead" at body is met by bringing the left shoulder forward and pressing the left arm close to the side.

A left hand "body blow" is nullified by keeping the right arm across the body, hand over the "mark," and at the same time drawing back the hips and setting the muscles of the thorax and abdomen.

A right hand "lead" at head is best parried by raising the left arm to the left front.

This is a favourite guard of Kid McCoy's. He has a playful knack of jerking his left hand downwards, after the completion of the "parry," across his opponent's jaw. Until he showed me this neat little hit I had never seen it. I want to see him show it to someone else now! One learns so much more from looking on; and dentists are expensive! It frequently happens that a man is driven into a corner and subjected to a rapid assault; he becomes bewildered and helpless for the moment. In such a case, temporary shelter

"LEFT HAND CROSS COUNTER."
(For "Left Lead at Head" with right hand covering face)

[See page 42.

from the storm may be obtained by sinking the head on the chest, shrugging the shoulders as high as possible, and throwing the arms across the body, right arm uppermost. This pose, if ungraceful, has, at all events, the merit of protecting the most vital parts, viz., the angles of the jaw and the "mark."

"RING" TACTICS.

QUITE as many contests are lost through bad generalship as through any other cause. It may be said that a good general in the "ring," like a good general in the Army, is "born and not made." Constant and intelligent practice, combined with sound instruction, will, however, produce a fair substitute for the natural article.

A good "ring" tactician must, in addition to experience, be possessed of a number of natural qualities in a high state of development.

He must be cool, cautious, and patient, quick to grasp an opponent's weak points; prompt and decisive in his measures to take full advantage of them. He must be cunning also, and full of artifice in leading his opponent to arrive at false conclusions concerning his own peculiarities.

He must know to a nicety his own powers of endurance, and be ever watchful for signs of faltering in his opponent.

Pluck, and the power of standing severe punishment, are, of course, of the highest importance. They are nature's gifts, however, and the want of them can only be discounted in a contest by immense scientific superiority.

The style of fighting adopted in contests or competitions must be adapted to the competitor's own peculiarities, with due regard to those of his opponent. For example, a strong, hard hitter, with a short reach, must "bore in" and keep as close to his man as possible, going for the body in preference to the head.

An active, quick man, with a good reach, should stand out and play at long shots, directing his attention principally to the head. It is good policy to take it easy for the first half of a round, concentrating all the work in the latter half. A judge, in marking the points of a round, is sure to be most impressed by what he sees last. It is well to commence a bout by several "feints" and "halt attacks," breaking ground constantly with a view to discovering the opponent's game.

Frequently, at a critical moment, by an assumption of carelessness or fatigue, an opponent can be induced to give himself away.

During the memorable battle between Kid Lavigne and Dick Burge, the former caught the latter napping with a very simple "dodge." Turning his head on one side, he rubbed his mouth with the back of his right glove. Burge at once

"HAMMER BLOW."
(When in-fighting.)

[See page 45.

dashed in to seize the apparently careless moment, only to receive a premeditated punch. For some time afterwards I saw this constantly tried by English pros., but the ruse was instantly recognised, and generally ended in the perpetrator's confusion.

Many bouts (mostly amateur) are thrown away by men failing to perceive their opponents are dazed, allowing them to recover, and the golden opportunity to slip by. Almost as many are lost by over-eagerness to knock a dazed opponent out. The latter is the graver fault of the two. A wild impetuous attack not only leads to breathlessness and inaccuracy, but frequently exposes the over-eager assailant to a fatal "counter."

Two dramatic instances of this kind are impressed on my memory: the first occurred at the Birmingham Club in 1898; the event was Plimmer v. Ware. Plimmer had all the best of the fight, and was winning comfortably on points. Towards the end of the last (twentieth) round, Ware, who was very weak, received a nasty blow on the chin, which staggered him against the ropes. Plimmer at once rushed in, keen for "blood." Ware, however, with a last "dying" effort, swung his right across, and catching Plimmer fair on the point of the jaw, knocked him clean out, and won the fight, just on the call of time. That little piece of unnecessary carelessness cost Plimmer and his backer a matter of £500.

The other case occurred during the Army Boxing Championship at Aldershot, in 1898. I forget the names of the combatants. The bout had hardly well commenced before one of the men was knocked off his feet by a terrific punch. It looked like a decisive "knock out." The fallen warrior, however, managed to stagger to his feet before the ten seconds were up. He was completely dazed and apparently helpless; so much so, that the referee stood up as if about to stop the fight. He fortunately hesitated, and the other man literally raced across the ring in his eagerness to finish matters. A distinct murmur of protest rose from the onlookers; but the "groggy" one, making a wild round-arm swing, his guardian angel guided his right hand to the angle of his opponent's jaw with fatal accuracy. This incident caused the greatest outburst of applause I ever witnessed, and it certainly was a curious sight. One man lying prone, absolutely insensible, and the other leaning against the ropes quite unconscious of what had taken place. In fact, as far as one could see, he left the ring without quite knowing who had been "knocked out." My advice upon such an opportunity as the above presenting itself, is, "Go for the opponent at once, and never leave him until he is out; but do so warily, and always precede an attack by a 'feint.' Hit as hard as possible, but above all things hit accurately." It is always desirable, if possible, to finish a bout without

"SLING CHANGE."
(Delivered during opponent's recovery from "Left Hand Lead.")
[*See page 46.*

"RING" TACTICS

leaving it to the decision of judges or referee. But it is both foolish and unnecessary to "mix things up" when winning easily on points. If decisively beaten on points, it is good policy to take all chances, and go for a "knock out."

DRAWING.—There is a species of tactics known as "drawing," the importance of which can hardly be over-estimated. It is well known to fencers under the name of "second intention." That is to say, making some premeditated movement to draw a particular attack from the opponent with the object of acting on that attack. This, in Boxing, would usually take the form of a "duck" and "counter." In fencing, of a "riposte."

This method is most likely to succeed—(1) with an opponent who has a fixed style and lacks variety, (2) with one who is constantly manœuvring to bring off a pet blow.

In the former case, e'er one round has gone by, it will be comparatively easy to foretell what the opponent's answering movement to each "feint" or attack will be. Say, for example, that the object is to bring off a right-hander on the face; working to within distance, make a short left "lead" at the head, and, always supposing you are fairly certain that the opponent will answer with a left hand "counter," "duck" slightly to the left, and follow with the right at the head instantaneously.

In the second case, the method is practically the same, and the "pet punch" will be all the more easily drawn if the opponent has already landed one or two successfully. The right hand body blow, as either an attack or "counter," is a favourite with many boxers. To draw it, get within distance, and, raising the left arm slightly, give the greedy fellow a peep of the coveted target, then "feint" with the left at the head, and, rapidly dropping the left arm to the side, receive the punch on it, at the same moment upper-cut with the right.

I saw a well-known amateur practically "knocked out" during a friendly spar by a pal, who caught him with this premeditated manœuvre. There is, of course, always the danger of misjudging the opponent's intentions, but the effectiveness of a successful draw is worth a bit of risk. I am very far from advising every one to attempt drawing tactics, because the instinct of divining an adversary's intentions is a gift which few possess. I may, perhaps, attach undue weight to it from the fact that it has practically won me every competition in which I have been successful, both Boxing and Fencing. There is an enormous intellectual satisfaction to be derived from persuading an adversary to act exactly as you wish, to his own disadvantage.

There is an old saw to the effect that "Continual dropping will wear away a stone," but, in order to produce any apparent effect, the drops should fall in succession upon the same spot. The moral, as

A "CLINCH."
(From a snap shot.)   [*See page 49*

far as Boxing is concerned, is obvious; having produced a tender feeling in the opponent's nose or short ribs, be as faithful as possible to the affected region. A succession of visits to the same abode paves the way to results far more rapidly than the same visits spread indiscriminately over a wide area. A very curious example of this species of "fidelity" was witnessed at the National Sporting Club, in 1899, during the contest between Jordan and Greenfield. Jordan practically confined himself to "ducking" underneath Greenfield's left arm, delivering each time two or three sharp taps with a hammer-like motion of the right hand over the kidneys. It produced little or no effect at first, and the spectators began to evince a certain amount of contempt for such apparently imbecile tactics. After a bit, however, Greenfield began to wince, showing signs of great distress, and finally was obliged to give in.

This particular game of "kidney punching" was at once adopted by other professionals, but it always ended in discomfiture. Thus we come to another old saw, "One man's meat is another man's poison."

It requires, however, considerable patience and tact to bring off a succession of blows on the same spot, for the simple reason that a man will instinctively protect a tender place. This instinctive anxiety may in another way, however, be utilized to his confusion. A really good "feint" at the sensitive locality is certain to produce an exaggerated protective movement, consequently an unusually large opening will be presented elsewhere. Good foot work is, of course, essential, and all boxers should constantly practice moving about a ring quickly, rapidly, and with as little exertion as possible. The feet should maintain their proper interval, and never be lifted higher than is necessary to clear the ground. The balance of the body must always be maintained, foot and hand working together.

When breaking ground, always work round the opponent's left, never to his right, unless when actually obliged to do so.

The order in which the feet are lifted and set down, whilst thus moving at an angle to the opponent's line of advance, is highly important.

When moving to his left, the left foot must move first, when to his right, the right.

If the wrong foot is shifted, the legs will momentarily assume the position of "astride," and the body be turned "square on" to the opponent.

This position exposes the whole target, and possesses no stability. If caught during the movement, a "knock down" is the almost certain penalty.

"Ducking" should be avoided as much as possible, except when "countering," as it is not only dangerous, but most tiring. Pedlar Palmer, the cleverest boxer in England, lost his fight with McGovern through a gallery display of unnecessary "ducking." A number of easy victories had made

"LEFT ARM GUARD."
(For "Right Hand Lead at Head.")

[*See page 50.*

"the Pedlar" over confident. I have seen him repeatedly stand within easy hitting distance, and make a series of perhaps four or five rapid "ducks," with the sole object of raising a laugh at his opponent's expense. He started a similar exhibition with McGovern in the first round, but the Yankee, placing his left hand on Palmer's right shoulder, guided his head into proper position as he rose from the final "duck," and knocked him out with a right-hander.

TRAINING FOR BOXING.

DURING the last 20 years our ideas on the subject of training have undergone considerable modification. In the old days, directly a man went into training, he was called upon to face not only a rigorous course of hard work, but a complete change in his diet and habits, and this, not by easy stages, but all in a moment. It is now generally accepted that a condition of perfect physical fitness must be approached gradually by a careful system of progressive exercise, a *perfectly* trained man reaching the top of his powers on the day of the contest. His diet, instead of consisting chiefly of half-cooked beefsteaks, is merely limited to good wholesome food, with plenty of variety. If he is accustomed to tobacco and the use of stimulants, these habits must be gradually moderated, and, if possible, given up altogether during the last fortnight. It is impossible to lay down exactly the amount of work necessary to make a man fit, as this must always be governed by individual considerations. The constitutions of men, as well as race-horses, vary very much, and the physical training necessary to make one man fit would cause another to break down or become absolutely "stale." It is the power of regulating diet and exercise to suit the individual that marks the first-class trainer.

"DOUBLE GUARD."
(When pressed.) [*See page 50.*

It is a common mistake to imagine that a state of absolute fitness, from an athletic point of view, must be one of perfect health. It is far from it. A man wound up to concert pitch, like a banjo string in the same condition, is perilously near breaking point. His blood, muscles, organs, and nerves are in an abnormal state, and although they may serve the immediate object in view, they must shortly be relaxed or give way.

It is after the period of training that the greatest care becomes necessary. As the approach to perfect fitness was gradual, so the relapse to a normal condition should be gradual. In the former case, there is the contest as an incentive and the watchful eye of the trainer as a restraint ; in the latter case, the trainer is no longer master, and there is every temptation to celebrate a victory or drown a defeat by over-indulgence.

There is no doubt that the Americans are a long way ahead of us in the art of training. I am quite convinced that English boxers, both amateur and professional, are, as a rule, over-trained. There is no worse fault than this. Directly a man passes the culminating point of physical condition, he loses dash and nerve ; he becomes listless and slow, and his brain, participating in the physical deterioration, his confidence, alertness, and readiness of resource become impaired. To my mind, the muscles of English professionals are, as a rule, too clearly mapped out, showing over-development fo r

Boxing, especially of the flexors. The men look as if their training had consisted of heavy dumb-bell work with a view to a weight-lifting competition. The development is uneven, and they look hard, stiff, and muscle-bound. It is a grave mistake to neglect a man's mind while tending his body. Physical and mental condition are intimately connected, and re-act on one another, consequently a man in hard training should have plenty of cheerful society and amusement. His exercises should be constantly varied, and every effort made to prevent his work becoming a wearisome labour.

Nearly every noted boxer has fads about training, and believes in some peculiar form of exercise as specially effective. For example, Charles Mitchell developed his legs and wind by running up the stairs of a lighthouse, while Jeffrys advocates "shadow dancing." Both these exercises are useful, but not essential, and in such cases it is good policy for a trainer to humour his client's fancies.

There are four exercises, however, which I think *are* essential, viz., Punching the Swinging Ball, Throwing the Medicine Bag, Skipping, and Sprinting. These exercises alone are sufficient to bring any boxer up to concert pitch. As the first two are comparatively modern, and, perhaps, not universally known to all amateurs, I purpose to deal with them separately, at some length.

"Right Hand Upper Cut."
(For Right Hand "Lead" at Body.)

[See page 62.

Roughly, the PUNCHING BALL teaches a man accurate, quick hitting, "ducking," "countering," and "slipping."

The MEDICINE BAG, swinging from the hips, and that happy co-ordination of leg, arm, and weight, so necessary in an effective punch.

SKIPPING, lightness and elasticity of movement.

SHORT SPRINTS, concentration of mind and muscle for desperate efforts.

I am far from advocating all training for Boxing being confined to these exercises alone ; on the contrary, the more variety the better. "Sparring" in moderation, to practise footwork, jumping, and free gymnastics are all good, but dumb-bells, gymnastics, climbing, and patent self-developers must be carefully avoided. I am not a believer in long, tiring, and generally dull walks, nor in long-distance running. A boxing contest or competition consists of a series of short bouts, where the pace is rapid and the intervals of rest frequent.

It does not seem reasonable, therefore, to test the patience and endurance of competitors by prolonged and monotonous work.

No trainer, who knows his business, gallops a sprint horse over a two-mile course. I am quite sure that long walks and runs tend to make men slow.

Most English professionals, when they go into training, seem to take it for granted that, as far as "ring" tactics and cleverness go, they have nothing to learn, and, consequently, confine themselves to the more or less mechanical process of getting fit.

It is most important, however, that a man in training should have constant practice with a varied assortment of boxers, not for loose play, but for the purpose of practising particular hits and manœuvres. If the opponent's style is well known, "stops" and "counters" for his favourite attacks should be assiduously practised.

Very early rising is to be deprecated, and on no account should violent exercise be taken before breakfast. All real hard work should be over by luncheon time. The hours for meals, for rising and retiring, must be regular, and medicine of any sort should be avoided as much as possible. Frequent baths are weakening. One in the morning is quite sufficient, but after hard exercise the body and limbs should be rubbed dry with clean towels, and be well massaged.

Before going into training, men should be medically examined as to soundness.

The teeth also should be put in good order, toothache being a desperate foe to physical condition.

It makes a great deal of difference to some men whether they are trained in a bracing or relaxing climate, and it is very often advisable to seek a change of air during the training period.

Plenty of fresh air is absolutely necessary ; bedroom and gymnasium, without being draughty,

BALL IN POSITION FOR PUNCHING WITH RIGHT HAND.
[*See page 81.*

should be well ventilated, and as much work as possible should be accomplished in the open air. The bowels should be free, sleep sound, appetite good, and mind cheerful.

THE PUNCHING BALL.

THE punching ball equipment consists of a wooden platform, an adjustable strap or rope, with a swivel at either end, and a large leather ball distended by means of a rubber bladder. The platform should be five feet square, at least, and consist of pitch-pine or deal boards, one inch thick, with cross pieces on the upper side. The platform should be raised about seven feet from the ground and be parallel to it. The strap or rope should be so adjusted that the ball will hang at about the height of an opponent's head.

The platform should not be erected in the corner of a room, but one side of it should be fixed to the wall, and the outside corners either held from above or supported by light wooden posts from the floor. I have found the ordinary punching balls most unsatisfactory. The bladders are constantly bursting, and the seams giving way.

An association football, largest size, is much more durable, and, before using it, the seams should be stitched inside by a saddler with a " herring bone " stitch. It will last a long time, and the bladder will never burst.

If the punching makes too much noise, a mattress or a couple of sand bags, placed on the top of the platform, will deaden the sound. When punching the ball, 4oz. gloves should be worn. All possible combinations of hits can be practised on this ball. It should always be struck when descending, and when the rope or strap is at about an angle of forty-five degrees with the platform. Beginners always make the mistake of standing too far away from the ball. It is well to commence by straight punching with the left hand. The ball, when at rest, should hang opposite to the left shoulder, and not more than two feet from it. It must be struck accurately in the centre, and the hand allowed to follow through after the blow, the shoulder being pushed well forward, and the body inclined slightly to the right after the blow is completed, to permit of the ball swinging back to position for another blow.

To punch with the right hand it will be necessary to shift a little to the left until the ball hangs opposite to the right shoulder, the hand "going through" as before, and the body being inclined to the left as the blow is completed. Having mastered the simple punches with right and left hand, all sorts of combinations can be worked out.

In training for a competition, the ball can be fought for the proper number of rounds.

The work should consist of short, sharp bursts at the highest pressure, and a rest should be taken directly the blows begin to lack vigour.

This is not only the most practical kind of exercise for Boxing, but is, at the same time, amusing and interesting work.

Many Military Gymnasia possess punching balls, and, whatever other apparatus may be lying idle, a punching ball never is. It is invariably surrounded by a crowd of eager "Tommies" waiting to "have a go."

There is a form of punching ball sold in many shops which should be carefully avoided. It consists of a light bladder, attached to floor and ceiling by rubber bands ; it affords no resistance to a blow, and is certain to teach the beginner that most vicious of all habits, "flipping."

THE MEDICINE BAG.

THIS simple but effective contrivance consists of a bag, or, better still, a small Association or Rugby football cover, half filled with maize. It should weigh about 8lbs. To use it, a correct boxing attitude must be assumed ; grip the bag loosely with the right hand, drawing the right shoulder back as far as possible, bringing the left shoulder well forward, and posing as if about to "put the shot."

Bracing up the right leg, and swinging the body from right to left on the hips, throw the bag, without any jerk, straight to the front, pushing the right shoulder well forward in doing so. The swing on the hips from right to left should be assisted by sharply drawing back the left shoulder. As the bag leaves the hand, the right arm should be fully extended to the front, the body leaning forward, the right leg perfectly straight, with the right heel raised off the ground. A similar exercise is carried out with the left hand. To save time and trouble in picking the bag up, it should be thrown to a friend to catch, so that it can be returned at once. This exercise is invaluable for developing the hitting muscles, and for teaching a novice how to throw his weight into a blow at the right moment.

The hitting powers of the famous Tom Sayers were developed by a precisely similar exercise, viz., heaving bricks into a lighter.

JUDGING.

THE fact that a man is a good boxer does not by any means ensure his being a good judge or referee, and this is equally true with regard to competitions in other branches of sport.

I know several first-rate fencers who are most execrable judges.

The best judges, however, are, or have been, first-class performers.

TOM SAYERS.

It is quite impossible to count every point during a round, nor do I know of a single first-class judge who attempts this. If he did, and restricted his decision to a question of simple arithmetic, the results would not be satisfactory. There are so many other points to be considered, such as the cleanness of the hits, the cleverness of the footwork, and the absolute fairness of the methods employed.

Then, if a man leading on points is almost "knocked out" once or twice, that makes a large hole in his balance credit.

Constant practice is, of course, essential, but this alone will never make a good judge where nature has withheld the necessary qualifications. Every man is liable to be prejudiced one way or the other, more or less, according to his temperament.

Suppose one of the competitors to be a judge's friend or acquaintance, either the judge's sympathies, and, with them, his marking, go with the friend, or his nervous conscientiousness leads him to mark his friend lower than he really deserves.

At any rate, he cannot have an open mind, and the justness of his decision, if he is honest, will depend upon his natural power of disassociating from his mind for the time being all impressions outside the actual boxing.

There are hundreds of ways in which a judge may be prejudiced. Some judges are inclined to side with the wishes of the audience, others, of a combative nature, to rule against the popular voice. Again, some boxers seem to have the power of gaining the sympathies of the spectators the moment they enter the "ring," others seem to repel them. It is only human nature to be biassed in favour of one or the other of the competitors, no matter what the contest may be.

It is usual, in a three-round competition, to allot seven marks to each of the first two rounds, and nine marks to the last round. In a glove contest, the same number of marks are allotted to each round. At the conclusion of each round, the judge or referee sums up in his mind the general result, and apportions the number of marks allotted accordingly. Here, judges must be careful not to allow themselves to be too much impressed by the points scored in the latter portion of the round, to the prejudice of the work done during the earlier portion.

Where the judges disagree, a referee can either give the bout to one or other of the men, or, if he thinks it a close thing, he can order another round. In the latter case, the judges must blot out of their minds completely what has gone before, and give their decision altogether on the merits of the last round.

Contests, in contradistinction to competitions, are decided by the referee alone. He should mark each round separately, and his decision should be guided absolutely by the total marks.

I think that during professional contests the marks should be posted up at the conclusion of each round. This would tie the referee down to hard facts, and prevent many a weak, hesitating man from giving a decision based upon the results of the last few rounds.

A referee should never take his eye off the men for a moment. He should be prompt and decided when his interference becomes necessary. A couple of warnings are quite sufficient for any man transgressing the rules. The third offence should meet with instant disqualification.

THE
NATIONAL SPORTING CLUB.

BOXING, both professional and amateur, can be witnessed in England with a degree of comfort absolutely unknown elsewhere. The Public Schools' Competitions, the Army Boxing Championships, and the Amateur Championships, are unique in their way. The two former are decided at Aldershot, and the latter at St. James' Hall, London.

The National Sporting Club, Covent Garden, is the home of professional pugilism.

The Club building is a magnificent one, containing reading-rooms, billiard-rooms, a dining-room, a gymnasium, and a theatre, and is, in itself, well worth a visit.

It was originally known as Evans's, a house of entertainment famous for its suppers, its music, and its dancing; like so many similar institutions, it gradually fell into disrepute, and, finally, was obliged to close for good and all.

The building afterwards passed into the hands of the Falstaff Club, who decorated it quaintly and appropriately. Most of these decorations are still to be seen, the walls, in many places, being adorned with life-size figures of characters from Shakespeare, beautifully worked in coloured tiles.

MR. JOHN FLEMING.
(Late Manager National Sporting Club.)

The gymnasium, which occupies the top floor, is delightfully original. It represents the corner of a street in "Ye olde London," the ceiling being painted to simulate a cloudy blue sky.

The old shops are faithfully represented, being built out from the wall, with old-fashioned gables, windows, and sign boards all complete.

It is truly a delightful change, after a hot bout with a boxing professor, to enter the old silversmith's shop, and find a luxurious modern bath-room. The boxing contests are held in the theatre, the padded ring being pitched in the centre of the stalls.

The theatre is a very handsome one, and can comfortably seat about 1,000 persons. The National Sporting Club was the outcome of the Pelican Club, and started business in 1890, with the late Mr. Fleming for its first manager. Since it opened its doors it has never once looked backward, and it can now boast of a long list of members, and a reputation for good management unequalled by any similar establishment in the wide world.

The Boxing season commences in October, and winds up in June. Every Monday night, during that time, the fortunate members and their friends can witness the best professional Boxing in the world in absolute comfort, and in the full assurance that nothing in the shape of rowdyism or disorder will be for a moment permitted.

So marked, indeed, is the orderly behaviour of the audience, that most American boxers feel nervous at first. They are accustomed to fighting in huge rough barns, and to being cheered or cursed by a perfect babel of tongues, and, consequently, don't understand being surrounded by rows of quiet men, mostly in evening dress, whose silence during the rounds is almost uncanny. If the papers are to be believed, "fouls" are frequent in boxing contests across the water, and many discreditable scenes are witnessed at the "ring" side. I have, however, seen many Americans fight over here, and their methods have always struck me as particularly fair.

One thing is quite certain : all professionals now know that, when competing at the National Sporting Club, the first shady trick means that its doors are closed to them for ever, and the spectators know that any misconduct will instantly bring the same fate upon themselves, be they peers or publicans.

It is well known that first-rate colonials will fight at the National Sporting Club for much smaller purses than are advertised in the colonies. These advertised purses have a nasty way of shrinking when it comes to a settlement, and the successful bruiser is surrounded by a horde of blackmailing sharks, whose hunger must be satisfied, if he values his safety.

At the National Sporting Club, the winner of a good fight, no matter what his nationality, is sure of an enthusiastic reception, and, what is more to the point, he is sure of the purse. The loser of a

MR. A. F. BETTINSON.
(Manager National Sporting Club.)

well-fought contest is received with a kindliness and sympathy frequently expressed in a practical form. One is always assured of a good night's sport at this club, because, if the fights set down in the programme should happen to collapse through early "knock-outs," there are always some useful pairs in waiting.

When I visit the National Sporting Club, I always make it a rule to dine there, for not only is the dinner good, and the waiting excellent, but the scene is full of life and bustle. I can imagine no more interesting spot for a student of character. All sorts and conditions of men are there, for as long as a man is "straight," can pay his way, and behaves properly, the management don't want to know by what exact line he is descended from Adam. At one table may be seen a "squad" of officers from Aldershot, at another a "block" of modest millionaire shirt fronts from the Kaffir market, at another a "field" of impoverished bookmakers fresh from the "ring," and here and there actors, jockeys, pugilists, and noblemen, all drawn together by the "Noble Art."

At 8.45 sharp an electric bell rings, and this heterogeneous crowd of humanity trickles slowly into the theatre; cigars and cigarettes are put out, and all settle themselves comfortably in anticipation of the real business of the evening. The establishment of the National Sporting Club has had an incalculable effect upon the morality of the "ring," and has, beyond all doubt, raised the tone of professional boxing enormously. It has, by its uncompromising attitude towards shady customers, induced a better class of man to enter the professional ranks, so that the professional pugilist of the present day stands on as lofty a platform of respectability as any of his brother pros. who make an honest living out of sport. During the many years which I have been a member of the club, I can honestly say I have never witnessed an unpleasant incident, nor have I ever seen a drunken man within its walls.

Such is the National Sporting Club, and yet it was gravely stated by an American paper, that Jim Corbett was about to purchase it, and run it on Yankee lines. To do Corbett justice, it must be added that he, with equal gravity, denied the soft impeachment. With as much reason might Tod Sloan be expected to buy "Hurlingham," or Admiral Dewey the "Naval and Military." To the energy, tact, and business ability of the late Mr. John Fleming, the National Sporting Club, in a great measure, owes its present unassailable position as the M.C.C. of Boxing. Mr. Fleming had all the characteristics necessary to a successful man; wonderful firmness and decision of character united with tireless energy, and a sharp eye to the main chance. His judgment in putting the right men together in boxing contests was unapproachable. He was universally respected during his lifetime,

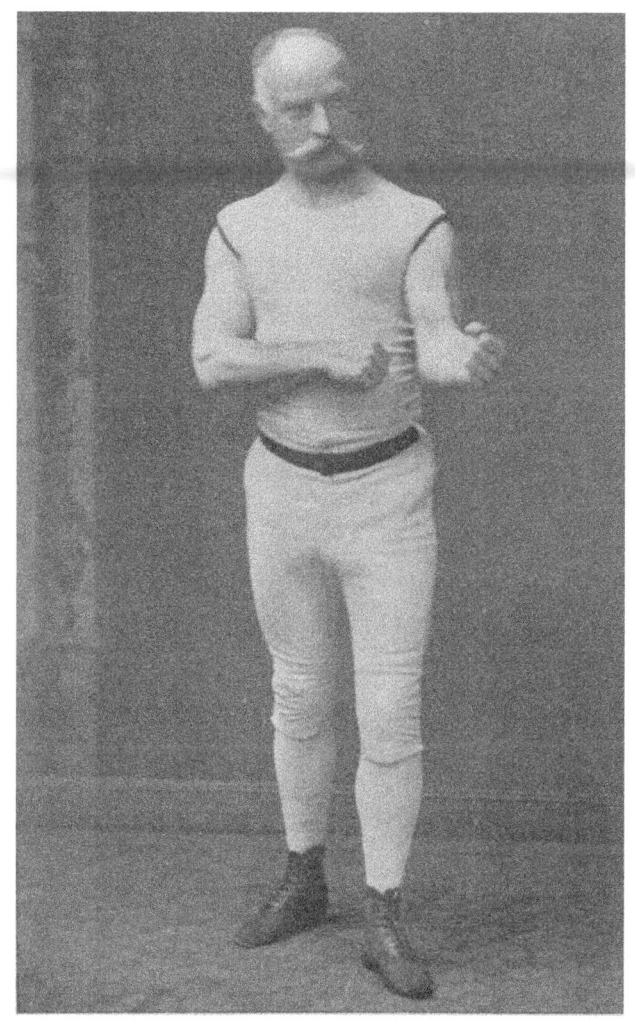

MR. J. B. ANGLE.

and his sudden death was deeply and widely deplored.

The Committee of the National Sporting Club are to be congratulated upon their acumen in selecting Mr. A. F. Bettinson to replace him. He has proved a worthy successor to Mr. Fleming, and the prosperous condition of the club at the present moment is the best proof of his ability as a manager.

Mr. Bettinson was one of the best amateur boxers of his time, having won the Amateur Championship in 1882, and was the happy possessor of a left hand punch which, for severity, was unequalled amongst professionals or amateurs. He is one of the best amateur swimmers of the day.

Mr. J. B. Angle is, without doubt, the greatest referee, living or dead, that ever controlled a boxing contest. So extraordinary is the confidence of the boxing public in his judgment and integrity, that I verily believe he could give the most scandalous decision without even the loser raising a protest.

No Lord Chief Justice or president of a general court-martial ever controlled a court with more dignity and firmness than Mr. Angle a boxing amphitheatre.

He has lately, unfortunately for the "Noble Art," retired from the "bench" : no other word adequately describes Mr. Angle's judicial seat. He is a stockbroker by profession, and I have no doubt that an echo of the "ring" can still reach him even amidst the "quiet" joys of "bulling" and "bearing."

Mr. G. Dunning, the well-known reporter of *The Sportsman*, has few equals, and no superiors, in his own particular line. His reports of glove fights are veritable "word pictures," which place in front of us every phase of a contest with the accuracy of a cinematograph.

His criticisms of the many knotty, not to say unpleasant, points which must necessarily arise in connection with Boxing, are invariably characterised by a wise moderation and strict impartiality.

Mr. Dunning, in his youth, was a famous "sprint" runner, and the smartness which was formerly lodged in his legs, has, luckily for *The Sportsman* and sportsmen, taken up a permanent abode in his pen.

MR. G. DUNNING
(of *The Sportsman*).

BOXING IN THE ARMY.

THE Army and Navy Boxing Championship Meeting, which takes place annually in the magnificent gymnasium at Aldershot, is now regarded as one of the great military functions of the year, second in importance only to the Royal Military Tournament. Indeed, amongst the men themselves, I am not sure that the gorgeous show at Islington is not looked upon as of secondary importance. The successful bruisers are the men most to be envied and admired in Tommy's eyes; after them come, perhaps, the regimental football team; and a long way behind, the crack rifle shots, bayonet fighters, and, I fear, even the happy possessors of the Victoria Cross. The pluck that can unflinchingly face severe punishment in the "ring" appeals more directly to the soldier's mind than bravery on the battlefield.

A "smack on the jaw" is always hanging round, whereas the bullets of the enemy seem far away. In most military stations a boxing competition is a sure draw, no matter how meagre the entry, or how poor the quality. It is one of the few forms of entertainment that can successfully compete with the attractions of the canteen.

If for this reason alone, Boxing ought to count the powerful blue ribbon party amongst its most ardent supporters. Indeed, no broad-minded man, with any experience of the Army and its wants, can possibly doubt the enormous support that any form of healthy exercise gives to the cause of morality and temperance. Boxing possesses many advantages over most other forms of sport, in that it is not dependent on the vagaries of the weather, requires no gear beyond a set of gloves, and can be carried out in a confined space. No recreation can possibly be more suitable on board ship. This the War Office have now recognised, and boxing gloves are supplied to every "trooper" for the amusement of the men.

I have frequently noticed that spectators depart after a boxing competition in a particularly quiet and sedate way; I mean more so than from other classes of entertainment. For instance, after a concert, the majority go out shouting, singing, whistling, or humming the airs they have just been listening to, but after a boxing show I have never noticed any desire manifested to reproduce the scenes of the arena. A good bout is an exhilarating sight, and I suppose a reaction sets in when it is over, making things appear dull, and depressing the normal mind a bit below par. This curious effect is decidedly in the interests of discipline.

I have always looked upon Boxing as the finest form of physical training and recreation that a soldier can indulge in. The preparation necessary for a competition is undoubtedly severe, but then it

BOXING FOR THE ARMY CHAMPIONSHIP AT THE GYMNASIUM, ALDERSHOT.

is distributed impartially, and is not in any way concentrated on particular groups of muscles, as in rowing, for instance. Given a good, sound constitution and a judicious trainer, no ill effects should ever follow. The legs are developed by using the skipping rope, and by both high and long jumping; the hitting powers by punching the swinging ball, the wind by short sprints, cleverness by light "sparring," and general health and staying powers by country walks, a generous diet, and regular hours. In following this *régime*, a man runs no extra risks of either breaking a bone or straining a muscle. In no other form of contest is staleness so absolutely disastrous; this is well known, and tends to prevent competitors overworking themselves. In addition to this all-round development of activity, strength, and science, Boxing brings out and fosters a number of fine qualities essential in a smart soldier—pluck, patient endurance under punishment, the faculty of quickly utilising favourable opportunities, judgment in knowing when to attack and when to retire, the power of controlling the temper, fair play, and humanity. Surely any sport which brings home to Tommy Atkins and his officers the fact that success depends upon this array of manly attributes, is a useful and elevating one.

Some time ago, Boxing received a severe set back through the nefarious practices of a few ruffianly professionals. The outside public began to look upon a pugilist and a blackguard as one and the same thing. This feeling naturally extended to the military authorities, who had not previously regarded the "Noble Art" with much favour. In fact, there was a very strong feeling that it was likely to breed bad blood, not only between individuals, but between regiments, and was generally hostile to the interests of discipline.

The Army Boxing Championship Meeting may be said to date from 1894, when it was for the first time held in the Aldershot Headquarter Gymnasium as a separate affair altogether from the Army Athletic Meeting. The meeting took place, as it were, under an official cloud. So bitterly opposed to it were some of the military authorities, and even a certain number of regimental officers, that at one time there was some doubt as to whether it would be allowed to take place. The untiring energy, however, of Colonel Fox, the Inspector of Gymnasia, carried the day, and, in spite of many gloomy forebodings of disorderly scenes and fatal results, the meeting proved an unqualified success. The Emperor of Germany, who happened to be in Aldershot at the time, together with his Staff, appeared at the "ring" side for a few moments. He was, however, only allowed to see a couple of exhibition bouts; this, I think, was a mistake, as, although he seemed to be very much interested in what he saw, he would have been very much more so had he witnessed a genuine contest.

COL. G. M. FOX
(Inspector of Gymnasia).

In spite of the admirable arrangements and the perfect discipline maintained at this competition, Boxing still remained in the official black books. But the clouds were soon to pass away. Lord Wolseley attended the Guards' Boxing Competitions in 1895 at Chelsea Barracks, and, in the course of a stirring speech at the close of the proceedings, he expressed his hearty approval of what he had seen. He said he regarded Boxing as likely to develop valuable and soldier-like qualities, and that for his part he would like to see "every soldier a boxer."

It is impossible to over-estimate the effect produced by this speech in the pugilistic world generally. It was reported in all the sporting papers, not only in this country, but also in America and the colonies.

It at once gave an enormous impetus to Boxing in the Army, removing every obstruction, and producing quite a boom in an art that had been languishing for want of a little official support. For some years previous to 1894, Boxing formed part of the principal military athletic meetings, viz., at Aldershot, the Curragh, and Portsmouth. These competitions were, however, carried out with very little method, and in a shamefaced kind of way. A ring was erected in the open, generally in some corner of the ground, by the simple method of driving in four pickets, and running a rope round them. No accommodation whatever was provided for the comfort of the spectators, the prizes were insignificant, and the men only half trained. A post entry was permitted, and I have frequently seen a spectator throw off his tunic and step into the ring just to have a go for the amusement of himself and his "pals."

Naturally, under such crude conditions, the majority of the contests degenerated into mere rough-and-tumble fights, where science was lamentably absent and "fouls" frequent. I know no more disgusting sight than to see two men, utterly out of condition, and without one particle of science, staggering about the arena covered in blood, like a couple of street rowdies, and this to the accompaniment of frantic yells from an equally ignorant audience. The Boxing also interfered seriously with the remainder of the sports, because it was carried on spasmodically throughout the day, and directly a contest was announced the men made a rush to secure places at the ropes, frequently crossing the running track during the progress of a race. Similarly, when the contests were temporarily discontinued, they rushed back to see the sports.

After the establishment of the Army Championships, the first man to come to the front was Sergeant Collins, of the Grenadier Guards. He defeated Private Ham (9th Lancers) in the finals of the Middle-weights in 1894, after a magnificent fight. Owing to an injury to his hand, he did not appear in 1895, but in 1896 he again carried off the

Middle-weights, beating Driver Pinchin (R.H.A.) in the finals. This was another grand contest, and was only decided after the referee had ordered an extra round. Collins, though not robust in appearance, was exceedingly clever, very cool, and possessed of wonderful staying powers. He has now retired from the Service, and is boxing instructor at the Oxford Gymnasium.

Drummer Collins, of the Grenadiers, was a smaller edition of his brother. He won the Light-weight Championship in 1896. A remarkable feat was accomplished that year by the 1st Battalion Grenadier Guards: their representatives carried off the championship in each weight.

Private Leahy won the Heavies, Sergeant Collins the Middles, Drummer Collins the Lights, and Drummer Philip the Feathers. These successes were, in a great measure, due to the keenness and vigorous support of the officers of the regiment, who organised a club of their own, which could boast of some three hundred members; the well-known professional, Alec Roberts, was engaged as instructor, and no trouble or expense was spared in discovering and developing regimental talent.

Private Ham, of the 9th Lancers, was a first-rate middle-weight. He, however, did not learn the art in the Army, being a professional boxer when he enlisted, known as the " Bermondsey Boy." He was a cool, strong fighter, with a nasty right-hand punch. His style, however, was better adapted to a lengthy contest than a three-round competition. This he proved by beating Sergeant Collins, of the Guards, in a ten-round contest at the National Sporting Club, after having been out-pointed by him for the final of the Army Championship. I recollect his first appearance at the Fire Brigade Sports at Aldershot.

He entered for all three weights. There was no weighing machine, but as it was apparent that the man weighed 11st. at least, he was not permitted to compete in the light-weight class. He seemed much disappointed, but it was a providential escape for the light men, as he won both the other weights with consummate ease, none of his opponents being in a fit condition to continue after the first round. He won the Army Middle-weight Championship in 1895, without any trouble whatever.

The final of the light-weights in 1894 resulted in a really first-class set-to between Corporal (now Colour-Sergeant) Kempster, of the Northampton Regiment, and Corporal Cooper, of the 7th Hussars. Kempster won. So close was the affair, that a purse was subscribed for a ten-round contest between them. This came off about three months later in the Concert Hall, Aldershot town. Cooper showed much more cleverness, and at the commencement of the last round had won comfortably on points. Kempster, however, made one desperate and final effort; he succeeded in landing the right on Cooper's jaw, knocked him out, and won the fight within a few seconds of the call of time. Cooper won the Light-weight Championship the following year, 1895, but afterwards went to pieces, being easily defeated by Drummer Collins at the National Sporting Club.

In 1895, the competitions were opened to the Navy, but only one bluejacket entered. This was Stoker Phillips, H.M.S. *Victory*, who was one of the veriest gluttons I have ever come across. He won a large number of competitions and contests at Portsmouth, for most of which I trained him myself. He was not clever, but was a terrific hitter for his weight, and could stay for ever. He ran up against a quick, clever man in the first round of the Army Meeting, and got beat on points. Before leaving Aldershot he challenged everybody all round to fight twenty rounds; an unfortunate gunner accepted, and Phillips had the satisfaction of knocking him out in the second round, at the Portsmouth Gymnasium. The last I heard of my friend the stoker was that he had defeated a big nigger in Jamaica for a £20 purse, a nice little thirst-quenching sum for a tropical climate.

Driver Pinchin, Royal Horse Artillery, appeared for the first time in 1896, when he got beat, as above described, by Sergeant Collins. He, however, won the Middle-weight Championship in 1897, after what was, perhaps, the best contest ever seen at Aldershot, with Private Smith, 10th Hussars. He was a very short, solid little chap,

with the cheeriest disposition in the world, and no
man could deliver a rib-roasting punch with more
graceful good humour. He generally fought for
the body, on account of his short reach. He was a
tremendous hitter, fairly clever, and could stand
more hard knocks than most men. This man
fought several times at the National Sporting
Club, and always acquitted himself well, even
when opposed to good professionals He has since
left the Army. Private Smith, 10th Hussars,
dropped from the clouds, or rather from the Cavalry
Depôt, Canterbury, in 1897. He had only just
joined the Army, and his name was quite unknown
in pugilistic circles. He was a Welsh miner, and
his only previous experience of the "ring" had been
some twenty knuckle fights in the mountains of
his native land. According to his description,
when two miners fall out, they go off with a small
following to some picturesque nook, and, having
stripped to the waist, fight away until one lies
down. These contests make a great demand on a
man's pluck and endurance, but they are hardly the
kind of training likely to lead to success at an
Army Championship; yet this man, by sheer
dogged determination and strength, very nearly
succeeded in defeating Pinchin, and I think he
would have, had there been another round to go.
He received the most desperate punishment in the
first two rounds, as he had no idea whatever of
avoiding it. He, however, stuck to Pinchin like a

CORPORAL SMITH.

bull dog, and in the third round the little gunner went very weak, his still smiling countenance showing serious marks of Smith's persistent attentions. Game as he was, I fancy the driver gave a sigh of relief when time was called at the end of that round. Smith defeated Pinchin in a six-round go a few months later at Dover. Corporal Smith has since come on in science, without having lost his other qualities. In 1898 he won both the middle and heavy-weights, a magnificent performance. He appeared genuinely distressed when I had to inform him that his opponents in the finals of each weight (owing to injuries) would be content with second money, thus giving him a double walk-over. Smith, who stands right foot forward, in my opinion is the best fighter the Army has ever produced.

In 1899, the entry fell just two short of the hundred, nine of the competitors hailing from the Navy.

The proportion of Bluejackets that enter for the Championships must necessarily be a small one, owing to the exigencies of the service, but those that appear are invariably well trained, and, although they have gained but one championship up to date, they always make a fine show and bring a refreshing air of good humour into the ring, which captivates at once the sympathies of the audience.

Corporal Smith, 10th Hussars, was unlucky in losing the Middles on a foul to Corporal Twyman,

13th Hussars, as the latter should, on several occasions, have been disqualified for deliberately falling in order to avoid punishment. Smith was lucky, however, in winning the final of the Heavies, on a foul, against Private O'Keefe, 2nd Grenadier Guards, who was leading well on points at the time. Smith, although still in the top flight of sloggers, does not strike me as being quite so good as he was the previous year.

Sapper Morgan, Royal Engineers, won the Light-Weights very easily, and was, undoubtedly, the best man who showed up at the meeting. He fights in quite the professional style, is very strong, and a terrific hitter for his weight. The officers' competitions brought to light no flyer, but Lieutenant Tudor, Royal Artillery, deserved great credit for his plucky attempt to win the Middles, after several exhaustive struggles in the Lights, which he annexed. He was, however, knocked senseless by Lieutenant Miers (Somersetshire Light Infantry), a much bigger and a fresher man.

In 1900, the record entry of 137 was secured, and no less than seventeen sailors competed, Seaman Skinner scoring the Navy's first championship by beating Private Roache, Grenadier Guards, after a magnificent fight in the finals of the Middle-Weights.

Owing to the war in South Africa, men belonging to embodied Militia regiments were allowed to compete, and the meeting, in point of form,

STAFF-SERGEANT SINGLETON.

numbers, and management, was the best ever witnessed at Aldershot.

Probably the most interesting bout was the semi-final of the Heavies, between the professional pugilist Dave Peters (Carmarthenshire Artillery) and Corporal McFadden (Royal Marine Light Infantry). Peters was, of course, a hot favourite, but he met more than his match in McFadden, who is a novice of magnificent build and great promise.

Lance-Corporal Saunders (South Wales Borderers) proved himself quite up to the best professional form, and, after a series of punishing encounters, found himself the gallant winner of the Light-Weight Championship. His best fight occurred in the second series, with Staff-Sergeant Dent, Army Gymnastic Staff, whose perfect muscular development, accentuated as it was by a network of quaint tattooing, excited the admiration of the audience.

Private Wheeler (5th Royal Fusiliers), winner of the Light-Weights, shaped well, and is much in advance of the average Army form.

As there were no delays, and all the byes were boxed off in an adjoining room, the competitions were finished in good time on the second day.

It is a curious thing that almost all the good boxers in the Army have been middle-weights; I have no way of accounting for it, and suppose it is merely a matter of chance. Staff-Sergeant Singleton, Gymnastic Staff, was about the best of the heavy men, although he never won a championship. In 1896, he was beaten by Private Leahy, of the Grenadier Guards, after a very close thing. Later on in that year he fought Private McKeon, of the Guards, at the National Sporting Club, the match being made for ten rounds. McKeon was a bigger and a better man than Leahy, but Singleton, who had come on wonderfully, was too good for him, and knocked him out in the eighth round, after a most exciting contest.

The officers' competitions have, on the whole, been rather disappointing, and, with the exception of 1895, the entries have been poor. The contests have been chiefly remarkable for the apparent want of condition of the competitors, copious bloodletting, and a prolific crop of black eyes. They are, however, immensely enjoyed by the spectators, as the average of "knock outs" is very high. This pleasing feature has been chiefly due to the persuasive right hand of Captain Graham, Royal Marines, who is a really good light-weight. He won the light-weights in 1895, and both the lights and middles in 1896 and 1897—a truly remarkable record. Captain Hulton, King's Dragoon Guards, winner of the middles in 1894-95, was a very clever middle-weight, with a very long reach.

Amongst the many good men the Army has produced may be mentioned Sergeant Warren, of the Guards ; Corporal Jordan, Royal Artillery (since turned professional) ; Corporal Scott, 15th Hussars ;

MR. TOM BURROWS.

Sapper Miles, Royal Engineers ; and Drummer Philip, Grenadier Guards.

No account of Boxing in the Army could be complete without mention of that marvellous all-round athlete, Mr. Tom Burrows, of Australia. From 1893 to 1898, this well-known and highly-respected professional was unofficially attached to the Aldershot Headquarter Gymnasium, and the successes of a large number of our military champions are due to his careful training and instruction. His assistance and experience have been of the utmost value to those responsible for the management of the Championship Meetings. He is Light-weight Wrestling Champion of Australia, holds the World's Record for Club Swinging, and is in the front rank amongst expert swimmers, runners, and jumpers. In addition, he is a man of high educational attainments, and a teetotaller.

Since the establishment of the first Army Championship in 1894, which was due entirely to the unaided energy and determination of the Inspector of Gymnasia, Colonel G. M. Fox, Boxing has made tremendous progress. At the present time, almost every military district holds its own meeting, and from amongst the winners selects and trains a certain number for the Championships.

In addition to these meetings, a large number of corps have competitions of their own ; foremost amongst these latter may be mentioned :—The

Grenadier Guards, the Royal Engineers, the Army Service Corps, and the King's Dragoon Guards.

The latter Corps are especially keen, and I have had the pleasure on many occasions of judging at their well-arranged and liberally-endowed regimental meetings.

The Army Champion Meeting owes its extraordinary success not only to the excellent arrangements on the spot and the perfect order maintained, but also, in no small measure, to the satisfactory manner in which the judging has been carried out. This truly important department has, from the start, been in the hands of the most able experts of the day. The names of Mr. J. B. Angle, Mr. Corrie, Mr. Smith, Mr. Dunning, the late Mr. Fleming, and Mr. Bettinson, are, in themselves, a guarantee of ability and impartiality which no one will question.

I think that all good sportsmen will agree that if the Army has done a good deal of Boxing, Boxing has done much for the Army, and that the man who has proved himself a good'un in the " ring " is little likely to prove otherwise than a good'un in the field.

AMERICAN BOXERS v. ENGLISH.

THE extraordinary successes of American boxers in this country, of late years, may well make us pause and endeavour to find out, by a careful analysis of their tactics, whence their decided superiority is derived. With the exception of Pedlar Palmer, the bantam-weight champion, and Dick Burge, the light-weight, it is almost impossible to put one's finger on a first-rate man in the United Kingdom.

At the present moment we are without a single man, in either the heavy or middle-weight division, with any pretensions to first-class form.

In instituting a comparison, be it understood that I take no account of the accident of birth, but look upon any individual as an American (in a Boxing sense) who has learnt the art in America. Nor must my remarks be taken as applicable to every English boxer, but to the majority only. The physique of the masses in this country has in no way deteriorated; on the contrary, everything leads us to believe that it has improved. At no time in the history of England has more encouragement been given to athletic prowess of all kinds, and any man, no matter how humble his origin or condition, can bring himself to the front, and become a popular hero by marked superiority at any of our national pastimes. Thousands of men are making their living out of cricket, football, running, rowing, boxing, etc. ; therefore, our lack of first-rate fighters does not proceed from want of good material, nor yet from want of liberal encouragement to physical development.

Anyone who has had the opportunity of witnessing the numerous contests between American and English boxers during the last few years, cannot fail to have observed a marked difference in the style of fighting and physical condition of the former when in the ring.

The Yankees, as we all know, are a wonderfully ingenious people, and their success in anything they take up seriously is due, in a great measure, to an absence of pig-headed conservatism, and a readiness to adopt anything new and give it a fair trial. They have given our ideas of race-riding a considerable shake up of late years through the unprecedented successes of American jockeys in the saddle.

They soon discovered many flaws in our system of glove-fighting, which trusted too much to grit and strength. These qualities, essential, no doubt, are out of it when opposed to similar qualities combined with the knowledge of "ring-craft" and perfect generalship that enables a man to rapidly appreciate his opponent's strong and weak points, and alter his tactics accordingly. The American fighter displays a marvellous knowledge of anatomy in his selection of tender spots, and the realistic "expression" which he imparts to his "feints" for an opening, forms an object lesson quite as important as the rapidity, force, and accuracy with which he gets "home."

Our English boxers are, with few exceptions, one-handed fighters—to put it roughly, they hit with the left and guard with the right. They all, more or less, adopt the same constrained position, with the weight thrown too much on the rear leg, left hand advanced and right hand held rather stiffly across the body in an attitude better adopted to "sparring" than fighting. In fact, the general pose is inclined to be cramped, consequently their movements in the "ring," such as "slide-slipping," etc., are awkward, and their balance is easily upset. They lack variety, especially in attacking, and make insufficient use of the right hand. Their pluck, however, is beyond all praise, and in this department they have no equals.

The American fighter is all variety; he moves about the ring lightly and rapidly, always perfectly balanced on his legs; his hands moving freely, almost carelessly, he is, as a rule, an admirable judge of distance, and reserves his strength for effective hits. He is, moreover, almost invariably a two-handed fighter, using his right freely, and trusting to a smart "duck" and a "clinch" to save himself.

Why in England we should insist on keeping the right hand so rigorously in reserve, has always been a puzzle to me. We give it the preference in lifting a heavy weight or when wielding a pen, therefore, it is the stronger and the more accurate of the two; why, then, not make more use of it in fighting? At the National Sporting Club I have frequently heard spectators remark, "So-and-so is waiting with the right," and he does wait, and goes on waiting until he gets beat without the wished-for opportunity having arrived. I do not, for a moment, advocate constant "leading" with the right, because it exposes the target too much, but I do say that our boxers do not use their brains sufficiently in order to make openings for it, as the Yankees do—and this, to my mind, is where they chiefly fail when opposed to Americans, viz., in the art of "feinting," and it is an art, as every fencer knows well.

A "feint," to be effective, must be so full of "expression" and reality, as to make the opponent shift his attentions to the threatened spot, and so uncover the real point of attack.

In bringing a man to the "ring" side in the pink of condition, fresh and full of life, with the right muscles developed in the right way, the Americans are undoubtedly our superiors. I have frequently seen English boxers completely over-trained, looking dull and listless, or having their muscles developed as if they were about to enter for a weight-lifting competition ; but I have never yet seen an

American enter the "ring" showing the slightest sign of staleness; their muscles have an "oily," supple look, and their movements a cat-like smoothness and rapidity, which plainly attest the judicious handling they have received. Good trainers are rare, and must have, in addition to a profound and scientific knowledge of their business, a natural aptitude for gauging the capabilities and constitutions of their men.

There can be no doubt but that our cousins across the water have made a deep study of this subject with regard to glove fighting, and the now almost universal use of the skipping rope, medicine ball, and swinging punching ball, by boxers of all nations, is a tribute to the practical outcome of their ingenuity.

Most boxers have their fads, or find that they derive most benefit from some particular form of exercise. Frank Craig, the celebrated "Coffee Cooler," believes in step dancing, and I don't know anything better calculated to make a man light and well-balanced on his feet. In his case the results are truly marvellous. I have seen most of his fights, and I never wish to see a more harmonious combination of grace, power, speed, and judgment. Dan Creedon once told me that, when training, his constant aim was to improve his capacity for keeping up supreme efforts whilst holding his breath, and there seems to be a good deal of sound sense in this.

To sum up, I attribute the superiority of American fighters to various causes :—

1. They are more scientifically trained, and, consequently, strip in better condition for the work before them.
2. Their free and unconventional style permits of more opportunities for a large variety of effective hits—this is especially applicable to severe upper-cutting with *both* hands. They make more use of the right hand than we do.
3. They are more carefully instructed in "ducking," "feinting," "clinching," "side-slipping," and foot work generally.
4. They have a much larger number of boxers to choose from.
5. A number of our most promising youngsters emigrate to America, owing to the superior money inducements held out to them.

CROCKET, THE PRIZE FIGHTER.

THE "KNOCK-OUT" BLOW.

It is only within the last ten or twelve years that pugilists have begun to realise the effectiveness of this particular hit. For its discovery we are indebted to America. Its development has gradually, but surely, revolutionised the style of fighting in professional contests.

There can be no doubt that the old-time prize-fighters were quite in the dark as to this scientific, humane, and summary way of disposing of an adversary.

The awkward cramped pose of the body and legs, together with the constrained way of holding the hands and arms, as illustrated in old engravings, point clearly to the fact that these men could not have had their minds concentrated on the "knock-out" as we know it. These old engravings of boxers, together with the published accounts of their tactics in the ring, give one a very accurate idea of the men's condition, the principal muscles developed, and the chief objects to which their efforts were directed.

It will be noticed that all these old heroes are depicted with the flexor muscles abnormally developed, especially the biceps of the arm. This was, no doubt, necessary then, because wrestling formed an important part of a prize-fight. But as far as quick, hard hitting is concerned, abnormal development of the biceps is a decided disadvantage. It produces a muscle-bound condition, by impeding the triceps (an antagonistic muscle) in its efforts to straighten the arm rapidly.

The ignorance of physiology and anatomy displayed by the average individual is truly astonishing. Nearly all boys, and a large number of men, seem to gauge muscular strength almost altogether by the size of the biceps. I presume that this arises from the fact that the development of this particular muscle is more apparent than that of any other, and also that it can with greater ease and decency be displayed for purposes of measurement and comparison.

The muscular development of the arms, however, has very little to do with severe hitting. The force of the true "knock-out" depends chiefly upon a swing of the body from the hips, in which the external oblique muscles play a large part ; towards the end of the swing, the extensor muscles of the rear leg are sharply braced, pushing the body forward, the swing movement being assisted by jerking back the left arm and shoulder. At the same time, the right shoulder must be shot forward to its fullest extent, and the right arm rapidly extended, with the back of the hand uppermost. The effort is a beautifully combined movement, in which the different muscles successively take their part, the whole weight of the body being thrown in at the moment of impact. On the completion of the blow, the right arm, body, and rear leg form a more or less rigid line of resistance.

The severity of the shock is enormously enhanced should the opponent be caught in a forward movement, in which case his own weight almost doubles its force. The blow must be delivered with lightning-like rapidity, and perfect accuracy on the side, but as near the point of the chin as possible, so as to take full advantage of the leverage of the jaw.

This blow is most commonly brought off, on the opponent's left hand "lead" at the face, by means of a right hand "cross counter," the left side of the chin being found whilst the muscles of the neck and head are in a state of tension from the effort of leading. The consequence is, that the neck experiences a sharp twist, which probably jars the *medulla oblongata*, and temporarily compresses the vertebral arteries at the base of the skull, thus checking for an instant the supply of blood to the brain; as a result, the man struck falls down in a dazed condition, and is unable to rise within the mercifully short regulation period of ten seconds.

I have on one or two occasions seen men "knocked out" by a left-hand blow on the right side of the chin, but this is quite a different hit, the effectiveness of which depends upon a short, sharp, half-arm swing, aided by a lifting movement from both legs, but the weight of the body cannot be thrown into it except by a man standing right foot in front.

The most dangerous, and infinitely the most painful, form of "knock-out," is that which is accomplished by a left-hand "hook" on the "mark," or, as it is sometimes described, "over the heart," that is to say, by a blow planted in the hollow above the belt and immediately beneath the breast bone. This was the blow with which Fitzsimmons disposed of Corbett in their memorable fight for the World's Championship. The popular idea, with regard to this hit, is that it knocks the wind out of one's body, and thus produces painful gaspings for breath. This, however, is not the case. A nerve called the *pneumogastric nerve* crosses this part of the body, and is connected directly with the heart. The blow sets up an irritation in the nerve, which is instantly communicated to the heart, temporarily checking its action, and, consequently, the blood supply to the lungs.

It is a very difficult hit to bring off, especially when using boxing gloves, because directly the opponent notices any movement towards the lower line, he instinctively sets his ribs and the muscles surrounding the threatened spot, protecting it at once from any serious effect—the size of an ordinary boxing-glove preventing the force of a blow from being concentrated upon a sufficiently small area. This "knock-out" can only be accomplished by a surprise blow, which gets home whilst the adversary's *intercostal* and *abdominal* muscles are relaxed.

The percentage of men fatally injured in boxing contests is absurdly small, and in this respect Boxing will compare favourably with almost any manly sport.

In England, within recent years, there have only been three fatal cases, and on each occasion it was conclusively proved in court that the victim was suffering from some vital disease at the time of the "accident." On one occasion, the unfortunate man actually entered the ring to spar a bye whilst suffering from pneumonia and a fractured jaw.

In the case of the man killed at the National Sporting Club, the *post-mortem* examination revealed the fact that he was in an advanced state of heart disease, and could not have survived any severe shock.

All managers of boxing competitions ought to adopt the simple expedient of insisting upon a medical examination of all competitors. In the case of professional contests, these examinations should take place before the men are put to the danger and expense of a severe course of training.

Some time ago, several letters were published in *The Times* from the head masters of certain public schools to the effect that they intended to withdraw their candidates from the annual schools competition at Aldershot, unless the "knock-out" blow was eliminated, as they considered that the display should be one of "science only."

As far as I can see, there are only two ways of doing this—

1. By ruling any severe blow a "foul."
2. By enlarging and altering the shape of the gloves, padding them all round to prevent the fist being clenched.

Rule 1 would result in endless disqualifications, while Rule 2 would introduce a new form of sport, which might be termed "The art of slapping." Personally, I should sincerely pity any boy brought up to look upon a system of this description as one of "self-defence," should he ever be called upon to protect himself in earnest. Much better prohibit Boxing altogether, and teach boys to rely upon some weapon in an emergency, than lead them to believe that, never having been taught how to deliver an effective blow in their lives, their fists are of the slightest use to them.

There is absolutely nothing dangerous or brutal in a clean "knock-out" blow on the chin. It certainly produces a temporary sense of dizziness, and in some cases a short period of insensibility, but it leaves no mark, draws no blood, gives no pain, and produces no objectionable after-effects.

THE "KNOCK-OUT" BLOW

In Boxing, the first and the most important thing for a beginner to learn is, to hit hard, to hit accurately, and to hit quickly, so that should he at any time be obliged to defend himself against an unskilled opponent, he can, upon a favourable opportunity presenting itself, either knock him out off-hand, or so daze him, that a repetition of the blow will close the affair.

PHYSICAL CULTURE AT PUBLIC SCHOOLS.

A GYMNASTIC, fencing, and boxing competition, open to all Public Schools, whose work is under the supervision of an instructor with an Army gymnastic certificate, is held annually at Aldershot.

These competitions are keenly contested, and are looked forward to with much interest by the different head masters, the boys, and the relatives of the competitors. It is a wonderful sight, which no one, who has the chance of seeing, ought to miss.

The form shown, both in the boxing contests and in the gymnastics, is of a very high order, and some of the exercises set would fairly puzzle an expert. The fencing has always been rather tame, and there is a large margin for improvement in this department.

Each school competing must be represented by two boys in gymnastics : may enter one only for each weight in the boxing competitions, one for the sabre, and one for the foils.

The huge Headquarter Gymnasium is, for the occasion, divided into two parts by a high wooden screen, on one side of which the boxing contests are held, and on the other the gymnastics and fencing.

The competitions come off on the Friday before Good Friday, and the building is always packed with masters, boys, instructors, and friends of both sexes, for whom luncheon is provided in a large tent pitched outside the Gymnasium.

The Boxing draws most of the spectators, and this is, I believe, about the only occasion upon which ladies can witness a serious exhibition of the "Noble Art."

It is amusing, and sometimes a little touching, to see a loving mother and sister complacently take up a good position close to the ring, to see "Tommy" or "Dicky" indulge in what they fully believe to be a harmless and graceful performance.

Presently "Dicky" appears, amidst a storm of applause, and proceeds to don an enormous pair of gloves. Mamma remarks, with much satisfaction, that they look "nice and soft," while sister "Maud" draws her attention to the "sweet looking" little boy with whom "Dicky" is going to play. Then "time" is called, and the "sweet looking" little boy catches Master "Dicky" a hot right-hander on the nose, which makes the blood spurt, and sends him staggering across the ring.

Mother and daughter, inexpressibly shocked, hurriedly depart, and wait outside the screen with pale faces and beating hearts. How they loathe the heartless spectators who can glory in this "brutal cruelty!" Wise papa, who has done a bit of "scrapping" in his time, is waiting at the competitors' door with a flask of brandy.

After a horrible interval of suspense, "Dicky" appears with a black eye, a swollen nose, and a cut lip, but beaming with smiles; contemptuously disdaining all sympathy, he graphically describes how he knocked his opponent out in the last round with a "crack on the jaw," and he seems to be rather doubtful as to whether he will ever recover or not.

With one breath, mother and daughter exclaim, "Serve the little beast right."

The above is, as nearly as possible, an accurate description of a scene I myself witnessed, and I have seen many similar ones. They are sometimes amusing, but generally make one feel inclined to jump into the ring and give "Dicky" a helping hand.

The boxing is generally over in time to give one an opportunity of seeing the wind-up of the gymnastic and fencing competitions. Then, the marks having been totalled up, the winning school is announced, and the successful boys come up for the Shield and Medals, amidst deafening cheers.

In 1898 no less than thirty-five Public Schools were represented at this meeting.

Curious to relate, the only school of any note which takes no part in this most sporting event, is Eton.

These competitions have, no doubt, done something towards popularizing gymnastics at our

Public Schools, and their value, as an advertisement alone, must be an inducement to head-masters to procure first-rate instructors. With one exception, every large Public School has some sort of gymnasium, with a qualified instructor in charge of it; yet, at the large majority, gymnastics is voluntary, and only a very small percentage of the boys attend the gymnasium regularly. During the summer months, most school gymnasiums might just as well be closed, for all the boys that make any use of them.

As a rule, a few boys, with some natural aptitude for apparatus work, are picked out and trained to a high pitch of efficiency, with a view to winning the schools' competition at Aldershot; to these few the instructor devotes all his time and energy.

The consequence of this system is, that the large majority of boys at most Public Schools receive no instruction in physical training whatever.

How such an intelligent body of men as the head masters of our Public Schools have failed to recognise the necessity of this all-important part of a boy's education, is more or less a mystery.

It is no excuse that they employ a highly-paid gymnastic instructor, have a fully-equipped gymnasium, allow liberal hours for recreation, employ well-known athletes as masters, or that cricket, football, rowing, etc., are made compulsory; for although all games, sports, etc., carried on in the open air, if indulged in in moderation, tend to make boys healthy, active, and manly, they do not, and cannot, compensate for the want of an intelligent and progressive system of Physical Culture.

For instance, of what use are either cricket or football to a weakly boy with an inclination, perhaps, to be knock-kneed, round-backed, or flat-footed? None at all. And if he is either forced or jeered into playing games, he is much more likely to grow worse than better.

There are, at this present moment, thousands of boys whose lives are being made miserable by being compelled to take part in sports for which they have no aptitude, and for which they are physically unfit.

It would be a splendid move in the right direction if every school adopted the system of training laid down for recruits of the Army, the efficacy of which can be vouched for by every officer commanding either a battalion or a depôt.

This system embraces a large number of marching exercises, free gymnastics, and setting-up drill. Precision of movement, smartness, and the proper carriage of the body, are insisted upon. The training is a progressive one, and includes a certain amount of simple apparatus work, jumping, and running. Its effect upon awkward and weedy recruits is truly marvellous. The slouching yokel is, in a few months, transformed into a smart soldier.

Every boy at school ought to have at least three hours a week of this work, delicate or awkward boys being placed in special classes.

These drills should on no account be awarded as a punishment, as this would at once have the effect of making the work unpopular with the boys; class competitions might be organised to encourage efficiency, and small prizes be given at the end of each term. There are plenty of smart instructors available, and the Army gymnasia are always open to head masters for purposes of comparison. As far as I know, the only Public School which has made any serious attempt in this direction is Wellington College.

Anyone interested in this subject, and wishing to see this system carried out to perfection by young boys, should pay a visit to the Duke of York's School, Chelsea. There the boys are clean, smart, and well set up, and the "ginger" and enthusiasm with which they tackle their work reflect the greatest credit upon their instructor, and all connected with the management of the institution.

GEORGE (KID) LAVIGNE.

Born, Bay City, Michigan, 1871.   Height, 5-ft. 3½-in.
Fighting Weight, 10-st.

Beat Jerry Marshall	10	rounds.
,, Andy Bowen	14	,,
,, Jack Everhart	20	,,
,, Joe Walcott	15	,,
,, Dick Burge	17	,,
,, Jack Everhart	24	,,
,, Eddie Connelly	11	,,
,, Joe Walcott	12	,,
,, Tom Tracey	20	,,
Lost Billy Smith	14	,,
,, ,, ,,	20	,,
,, G. McFadden	19	,,

Lavigne is the cleverest fighter I have ever seen. He is a wonderful master of "ring-craft," and as quick as lightning on his feet. His tactics are short rushes and double "leads."

KID LAVIGNE.

PEDLAR PALMER.

Born, Canning Town, November 19th, 1876. Height, 5-ft. 3-in. Fighting weight, 8-st. 2-lbs.

Beat Walter Croot	17	rounds.
,, Ernie Stanton	20	,,
,, Billie Plimmer	14	,,
Draw George Dixon	6	,,
Beat Johnny Murphy	20	,,
,, Ernie Stanton	15	,,
,, Dave Sullivan	20	,,
,, Billie Plimmer	17	,,
,, Billy Rutherford	3	,,
Lost Terry McGovern	1	,,
Beat Harry Ware	15	,,
Lost ,, ,,	20	,,

Pedlar Palmer has a wonderful record. I have witnessed almost all his fights. The rapidity of his leading and "ducking" is absolutely marvellous. His style, however, is lacking in freedom, and he is not a punishing hitter. He always gives one the impression that he is "sparring" for exhibition.

PEDLAR PALMER.

FRANK CRAIG

(THE COFFEE COOLER).

Born, New York, April 1st, 1870.   Height, 5-ft. 10¾-in.
Fighting weight, 11-st. 4-lbs.

Lost Billy McCarthy	4	rounds.
,, Steve O'Donnell	4	,,
Beat Billy McCarthy	6	,,
,, Joe Butler	6	,,
,, Fred Morris	18	,,
,, Bill Slavin	4	,,
Lost Peter Maher	2	,,
Beat J. O'Brien	2	,,
,, Ted Pritchard	1	,,
,, J. O'Brien	1	,,
Lost Frank Slavin	1	,,
,, Dan Creedon	20	,,
Beat Tom Duggan	12	,,
Lost Dick O'Brien	2	,,
Beat Billy Edwards	12	,,
,, George Crisp	13	,,
Lost Tommy Ryan	10	,,
,, Jack Root	6	,,
,, Tommy West	14	,,
,, George Gardner	5	,,

Craig has fought more fights than probably any other man in the "ring." He is a good-looking coloured man, most beautifully proportioned. He has a long reach, and is a desperately hard hitter. He is one of the most respectable men in the "ring," and the fairest or fighters.

FRANK CRAIG ("THE COFFEE COOLER").

BOB FITZSIMMONS.

Born, 1862, at Helston, Cornwall.   Height, 5-ft. 11¾-in.
Fighting weight, 12-st.

Beat Billy McCarthy	9	rounds.
,, Jack Dempsey	13	,,
,, Peter Maher	12	,,
,, Joe Godfrey	1	,,
,, Jim Hall	4	,,
Draw Joe Choynski	5	,,
Beat Dan Creedon	2	,,
,, Peter Maher	1	,,
Lost (foul) Tom Sharkey	8	,,
Beat J. Corbett	14	,,
(World's Championship).		
Lost J. Jeffries	11	,,
(World's Championship).		
Beat Jeff Thorne	1	,,
,, Gus Ruhlin	6	,,
,, Tom Sharkey	2	,,

Fitzsimmons is, in the opinion of the best judges, in spite of his defeat by Jeffries, not only the finest fighter of the day, but the finest fighter that ever donned a "mitten." Possessed of almost superhuman endurance and desperate punishing power, he shuffles about the ring with ungainly rapidity, and as he is now almost 40 years of age, this hairless and solitary upholder of England's honour amongst heavy-weight professionals, must have a constitution as hard as the rocks of his native Cornwall.

BOB FITZSIMMONS.

JAMES J. JEFFRIES.

Born, 1875.   Height, 6-ft. 1½-in.

Beat Gus Ruhlin	20	rounds.
Draw Joe Choynski	20	,,
Beat Joe Goddard	4	,,
,, Peter Jackson	3	,,
,, Tom Sharkey	20	,,
,, Bob Armstrong	10	,,
,, Bob Fitzsimmons	11	,,
,, Tom Sharkey	25	,,
,, Jem Corbett	23	,,

Jeffries is the biggest and most powerful man that ever won the World's Championship.

JAS. J. JEFFRIES.

TOM SHARKEY.

Born, Dundalk, Ireland, November 26th, 1873. Height, 5-ft. 8½-in.

Beat Sailor Brown	2	rounds.
,, Joe Choynski	8	,,
Draw J. Corbett	4	,,
Beat Bob Fitzsimmons (on a foul)	8	,,
Draw Peter Maher	7	,,
Beat Joe Goddard	6	,,
Lost J. Jeffries	20	,,
Beat Gus Ruhlin	1	,,
,, J. Corbett (on a foul)	9	,,
,, Kid McCoy	10	,,
Lost J. Jeffries	25	,,
,, Gus Ruhlin	15	,,

Sharkey is a true bull-dog — short, enormously powerful, and possessed of wonderful powers of endurance.

TOM SHARKEY.

BOXING RULES

OF THE

NATIONAL SPORTING CLUB.

1.—In all competitions the ring shall be roped, and shall be not less than 12 feet, or more than 18 feet, square.

2.—Competitors to box in light boots or shoes (without spikes) or in socks, and to weigh on the day of competition in boxing costume without gloves. No gloves to weigh less than 4 ozs. each.

3.—In all competitions the number of rounds to be contested shall be three. The duration of each of the first two rounds shall be three minutes, and of the third round four minutes; and the interval between the rounds shall be one minute.

4.—In all special contests, the number of rounds shall be specified; the duration of each round shall be three minutes, and the interval between the rounds shall be one minute. No contests for endurance shall be permitted.

5.—In all competitions any competitor failing to come up when time is called shall lose the bout.

6.—A competitor who draws a bye shall be bound to spar for the specified time with any opponent approved by the judges.

7.—A competitor shall be entitled to the assistance of two seconds only, whose names shall be submitted to the Committee for approval. The seconds shall leave the ring when time is called, and shall give no advice or coaching to the competitors during the progress of any round.

8.—If a competitor is knocked down, he must get up, unassisted, within ten seconds, his opponent meanwhile retiring out of striking distance. A competitor failing to resume the contest at the expiration of ten seconds, will be considered defeated.

9.—In all competitions, a timekeeper shall be appointed. Results shall be decided by two judges and a referee, who shall be stationed apart. The judges shall award in competitions of three rounds, at the end of the first and second rounds, five marks, and at the end of the third round, seven marks, to the best man, and a proportionate number to the other competitor ; but in competitions of longer duration, the maximum number of marks to be allotted shall be five for each round. At the end of each bout the judges' papers are collected by an official appointed for that purpose. In cases where the judges agree, such official shall announce the name of the winner; but in cases where the judges disagree, such official shall so inform the referee, who shall thereupon act according to Rule 10.

10.—The referee shall have power to give his casting vote when the judges disagree, or he can order a further round limited to either two or three minutes.

11.—The decision of the judges or referee, as the case may be, shall be final, and without appeal.

12.—In all competitions, the decision shall be given in favour of the competitor who obtains the greatest number of points. The points shall be for "attack": direct, clean hits with the knuckles of either hand on any part of the front or sides of the head, or body above the belt; "defence": guarding, slipping, ducking, counter hitting, or getting away. Where points are otherwise equal, the preference to be given to the competitor who does most of the leading-off, or who displays the best style.

13.—The referee may disqualify a competitor for delivering a foul blow, whether intentionally or otherwise, or for butting, shouldering, or wrestling, and he may also, after giving due caution, disqualify any competitor who is boxing unfairly, by flicking, or hitting with the open glove, by hitting with the inside or butt of the hand, the wrist, or elbow, or by roughing at the ropes.

14.—If, in the opinion of the referee, a deliberate foul is committed by a competitor, such competitor shall not be entitled to any prize.

15.—The breaking of any of these rules by a competitor, or his seconds, shall render a competitor liable to disqualification.

16.—The judges and referee shall decide (1) any question not provided for in these rules ; (2) the interpretation of any of these rules.

A Selection Of Classic Instructive Titles Relating To The Art Of Pugilism & Self Defence In Both War & Peace
Find our entire selection @ naval-military-press.com

ALL-IN FIGHTING
The distilled knowledge of W.E. Fairbairn, legendary SOE instructor in unarmed combat, and inventor of the Sykes-Fairbairn knife, who learned his deadly skills in 30 years on the Shanghai waterfront. Fully illustrated.
9781847348531

ART OF BOXING AND SCIENCE OF SELF DEFENCE
Former Lightweight Champion Billy Edwards shares the techniques and strategies of the sweet science in his beautifully illustrated boxing guide. Explore boxing's transition from bare knuckle spectacle to today's Marquis of Queensbury ruleset.
9781474539548

SELF DEFENCE OR THE ART OF BOXING

Ned Donnelly was a pioneer of boxing training during the late Victorian era. Explore the strategies and techniques used by this trainer of champions via a series of easy-to-follow illustrations and clear, concise coaching steps.

9781474539562

JACK GOODWIN'S BOXING

This 1920's boxing masterpiece by Jack Goodwin puts you in the shoes of a coach in that era. Uncover the best ways to run, manage and train boxers as taught by Jack Goodwin, a champion and trainer of champions in the noble science.

9781474539586

THE COMPLETE BOXER

Gunner Moir provides detailed instructions on the techniques he deployed to become British Heavyweight Champion. Taught in a series of easy to learn techniques, combinations, and boxing strategies.

9781474539609

ART OF WRESTLING

George de Relwyskow Army Gymnastic Staff

In the appreciation to this book Captain Daniels, V.C., M.C., Rifle Brigade, states: "In adding a word to this book on the style of wrestling as taught at the Headquarters Gymnasium of the British Army, and having had personal experience in the various holds and throws taught, I consider it has been of great value in the training of the soldier, and the bringing out of those qualities of grit and determination which have been seen in all ranks who have taken an active part throughout the greatest war in history." 1919.

9781783313563

KILL OR GET KILLED

Rex Applegate's "kill or be killed" helped prepare America's marines, soldiers, sailors, spies and airmen for the realities of war. This highly shared and respected work provides all you need to know about unarmed combat and close quarter engagement with the enemy.

9781474539661

BOXING (V-Five)
The Aviation Training Office of the Chief of Naval Operations
The game-changing V-Five suite of training manuals helped get a generation of American aviators fit for war. Here we explore how the airmen of the US navy trained in boxing as part of their military fitness regime.
9781474539623

THE TEXTBOOK OF WRESTLING
Get your wrestling skills matt-ready from wrestling champion and world-renown trainer Ernest Gruhn. Replete with detailed holds, throws, pins and strategies for success in a wide range of wrestling rulesets.
9781474539647

MANUAL OF PHYSICAL TRAINING 1914
(United States Army)
Published just prior to the outbreak of World War 1, this beautifully illustrated guide was designed to revolutionise the combat fitness and readiness of the US Army covering a wide range of gymnastic and combat calisthenic exercises.
9781474539708

DEAL THE FIRST DEADLY BLOW
United States Department of the Army
This Vietnam-era classic showcases in detail how the US Forces trained in close quarter combat. Known as the "encyclopaedia of combat" it helped a generation learn how to become devastating effective with empty hands, knives and bayonets alike.
9781474539722

HAND-TO-HAND COMBAT
Bureau of Aeronautics U.S Navy 1943
This is one of the best combative manuals from World War 2, developed by the US Navy V-Five Staff, that included the renowned American wrestler Wesley Brown. It is then not especially surprising that wrestling skills predominate in this manual, and form the base skill-set for this combative system.
9781474537391

ABWEHR ENGLISCHER GANGSTER METHODEN DEFENSE OF ENGLISH GANGSTERS METHODS – SILENT KILLING – FULL ENGLISH TRANSLATION
In 1942 the Wehrmacht published a training manual with the goal of countering the "silent killing" tactics used by the British commando units. The manual was – much in line with typical National Socialist terminology –titled "Abwehr Englischer Gangster-methoden" or "Defence Against English Gangster methods".
This book was compiled due the Wehrmacht intelligence operatives uncovering of a British hand-to-hand course for the SOE, Commandos, et al, on methods of quick and silent killing (undoubtedly developed by W. E. Fairbairn and E. A. Sykes). They correctly assessed that their troops in general and particularly the Geheime Staatspolizei (Gestapo), Sicherheitsdienst (SD), their security guards, and sentries would be in grave danger when confronted by men trained in these methods. This manual/program was the Wehrmacht's response.
9781474538336

BOXING FOR BOYS

Regtl. Sergt.-Major E B Dent Army Gymnastic Headquarters
A successful system of boxing instruction for large classes, to allow tuition with no detriment to the "backward or shy pupil". Covers Kit-On, Guard-Sparring-Advance-Point & Mark-Ducking-Medicine, Bag-Left & Right Hooks etc. The author considered that boxing systematically taught to the youth was beneficial exercise, and would have a marked elevating influence on the national character.

9781783314607

HAND-TO-HAND FIGHTING

A System Of Personal Defence For The Soldier (1918)
A tough book on the art of hand to hand fighting in the trenches of the Great War. Demonstrating techniques utilised to "do away with the enemy", many of which are barred in clean wrestling, the book includes good clear photographic illustrations presenting important attack methods including the "Hammer Lock", "Kidney Kick", "Head Twist", "Knee Groin Kick", and the "Knee Break", all very important in a man to man, life or death encounter, when fighting in the mud of the trenches.

9781783313983

HAND TO HAND COMBAT

Francois d'Eliscu taught thousands of U.S. Army Rangers how to fight down and dirty in World War II. d'Eliscu doesn't get the press that Fairbairn and Applegate do, but he did a commendable job writing this book. It is basic, meant for training raw recruits in a short amount of time before sending them to the front, but simple is good when you are in combat, as most combative experts' will tell you.

9781474535823

COLD STEEL

A cold-war combatives classic. John Styers, US Marine and WW2 veteran, lays out his approach to close quarters combat with rifle, bayonet, stick, knife and empty hands. Explore what helped wartime and post-war Marines stay ahead of the competition with lucid imagery and clear combative descriptions.

9781474540643

THE COMPLETE KANO JIU-JITSU

Join world-famous physical culture expert H. Irving Hancock, and Jiu-Jitsu specialist Katsukama Higashi as they showcase the art of 'Kano Jiu-Jitsu' now known as Judo. Get an exclusive glimpse into the transitional era of the martial art, alongside how it uses Japanese physical culture methodologies for self-improvement.

9781474540735

W.E. Fairbairn's Complete Compendium of Lethal, Unarmed, Hand-to-Hand Combat Methods and Fighting In Colour

All 844 images of Fairbairn and his assistants can now for the first time be seen in full colour, lending a clarity to the practical methods of mastering the manner of dealing with an assailant, both in time of war and when placed in difficulty during unpleasant modern urban situations. These various holds, trips, kicks, blows etc, allow the average man or woman a position of security against almost any form of armed or unarmed attack.

Captain W.E. Fairbairn would have approved of this new colour version, that gives an illustrative clarity to the original that was lacking in previous monochrome reprints of his work.

All six of W.E. Fairbairn's works in one binding to create the ultimate colour compendium: Get Tough-All-In Fighting-Shooting to Live-Scientific Self-Defence-Hands Off!-Defend

9781783318735

SELF DEFENCE FOR WOMEN COMBATO

Join the Canadian combatives legend William "Bill" Underwood as he showcases self-defence for women. Over the course of clear photography, sketches and instructions he lays out a curriculum for self-defence for the attacks women would be most likely to face.

9781474540711

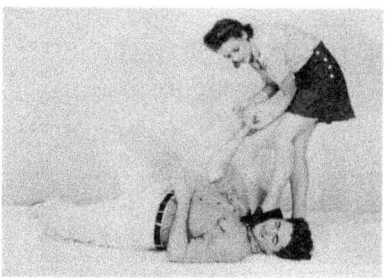

SCIENTIFIC UNARMED COMBAT
The Art of Dynamic Self-Defence

Learn the esoteric Sri Lankan art of 'Cheena-Adi' with R. A Vairamuttu. This guide explores armed and unarmed self-defence drawing heavily from Indian martial culture, alongside wellness and development from Indian physical culture, fitness, diet and medicine.

9781474540728

THE NEW SCIENCE
Weaponless Defence

Join wrestling champions Prof F. S Lewis, William V Gregory and Boxing Champ Tommy Burns as they showcase street orientated self-defence from people with a proven track record of fighting success. This 1906 manual via a series of photos and instructions lays out simple, tried and tested ways to keep yourself safe.

9781474540704

COMBAT CONDITIONING MANUAL
Jiu-Jitsu Defence, Bayonet Defence and Club Defence

This 1942 guide for marines lays out the basics of combat Ju Jitsu as part of an overall training regimen for US Marines. It's a holistic guide that covers defences against armed and unarmed attackers, physical fitness and even first aid.

9781474540698

BOXING TAUGHT THROUGH "SLOW MOTION FILM"

Learn the ropes from the best fighters of the 1900s-1930s in this unique boxing manual. Using stills from super slow-mo fight footage, this treasure trove unpacks the skills, tips and tactics of the champs for you to emulate at home.

9781474540681

HOW TO BOX CORRECTLY

Explore the art of boxing according to famous Bronx boxing brand Ben Lee in this 1944 how-to guide. Learn the ropes from one of the nation's top trainers and boxing journalists John J. Romano, in this warmly illustrated guide to the sweet science.

9781474540674

THE ART OF IN-FIGHTING BY FRANK KLAUS

German-American Middleweight Champ Frank Klaus showcases his KO-scoring boxing IQ in this 1913 guide. Containing clear and easy to understand photography and descriptions, Klaus gives us an insight into the emerging hard-hitting American style of professional boxing.

9781474541473

THE ART OF BOXING AND HINTS ON TRAINING

Crafted just after WW1 in 1919, this guide by Royal Naval Physical Training, Chief Staff Instructor J.O'Neil explores the military benefits of boxing. Showcasing via lucid text and full page photography.

9781474541510

JIM DRISCOLL'S TEXTBOOK OF BOXING

Driscoll was a former Featherweight World Champion and in this 1914 guide, he uses cutting edge and clear photography to showcase the new scientific boxing method. Driscoll showcases to the audience the way to best combine British and American boxing training and fighting philosophy.

9781474541466

JUDO AND ITS USE IN HAND TO HAND COMBAT FROM SEABEES NAVAL ENGINEERING CORPS

Brought to you by William Caldwell of the Seabees Naval Engineering Corps. This WW2 close combat classic provides an insight into the "Combat Judo" used by the navy to prepare personnel for the dangers of theatre. Fully photographed and accessible with clear instructional content to follow.

9781474541480

AMERICAN JUDO ILLUSTRATED

Brought to you by William Caldwell of the Seabees Naval Engineering Corps. This WW2 close combat classic provides an insight into the "Combat Judo" used by the navy to prepare personnel for the dangers of theatre. Fully photographed and accessible with clear instructional content to follow.

9781474541527

HAND TO HAND COMBAT – Field Manual 21-150

An example of Cold War / Korean War close combat training. Filled with instructor notes and clear imagery covering unarmed and "cold weapon" combat such as bayonet, knife and garrotte.

9781474541459

BOXING

This 1906 guide from former English Heavyweight Champion Captain Johnstone, showcases the leading techniques, skills, strategies and fighting philosophies of the day. Brought to life with vivid storytelling from military boxing advocates alongside lucid photography and crisp follow-along guidance for boxers to follow.

9781474541534

KILL OR GET KILLED

Lt Col. Rex Applegate's WW2 Combat Classic 'Kill or Get Killed' is one of the most detailed and comprehensive guides of armed and unarmed combat ever written. From unarmed, to knife, bayonet, pistol, garotte and more – Applegate provides written descriptions, photographs, illustrations on more to showcase and share the skills of forces like the O.S.S.

9781474541541

BALL PUNCHING – A PICTORIAL GUIDE TO THE SPEEDBAG

This 1922 guide from Tom Carpenter is a response to the 'speedbag' craze of the early part of the century. It showcases via clear instructions and photography how to best use tools such as maize, speed and double-end bags for fitness and fighting skills.

9781474541503

SCIENTIFIC BOXING FROM A FISTIC EXPERT
Diet – Fight Training – K.O. Punching

This 1937 guide to the American school and style of professional boxing provides a clear and well-illustrated suite of technical skills and drills to compete successfully. Replete with training advice, rule guidance and ring Generalship principles to help boxers be inline with the latest advice and training acumen.

9781474541497

www.ingramcontent.com/pod-product-compliance
Lightning Source LLC
Chambersburg PA
CBHW050013090426
42734CB00020B/3256